1973

The Merrill Studies
in
Moby-Dick

CHARLES E. MERRILL STUDIES

Under the General Editorship of
Matthew J. Bruccoli and Joseph Katz

The Merrill Studies
in
Moby-Dick

Compiled by

Howard P. Vincent
Kent State University

Charles E. Merrill Publishing Company
A Bell & Howell Company
Columbus, Ohio

Standard Book Number: 675-09448-8

Library of Congress Catalog Number: 72-93047

1 2 3 4 5 6 7 8 9 10 — 78 77 76 75 74 73 72 71 70 69

Printed in the United States of America

Preface

The amount of writing now accumulated on Moby-Dick—more than 500 articles, many books, and countless short commentaries —is sufficient to stagger any student of literature. It is of a magnitude appropriate to the great whale himself, and, as Melville said of the White Whale, it is "ubiquitous in time and place."

Such a wealth of secondary material frustrates the anthologist as well, who must from this rich smorgasbord of words arbitrarily select a menu which will nourish the reader's constitution, delight his palate, but not overcrowd his plate. A word, then, is in order about the structure of the present collection.

"Loomings" (Part I) is a selection of five favorable reviews which were written immediately upon publication of *Moby-Dick*. These reviews are exceptional since they are in contrast, even opposition, to most of the rest of the contemporary reviews, which panned the book, and since four of these five were written by men of distinction in American letters. Even though they were voices crying in a wilderness, they well expressed value judgments which, a century later, the world would re-echo and which subsequently the plodding scholars (see Part III) would carefully establish.

"The Advocate" (Part II) reprints three fine essays—also lone voices in a more desolate wilderness—written during the decades when Melville's reputation had dimmed to mere citation and when histories of literature even neglected to name *Moby-Dick* as one of his books. MacMechan's advocacy (1899) is a landmark all must honor. The Lawrence essay (1923) is justly famous, but it bears

v

repeated readings and is printed here with the long quotations from *Moby-Dick* deleted, then necessary because then unknown. The Colcord essay (1922) is in my opinion one of the two or three finest testimonies to *Moby-Dick* ever written, especially valuable as coming from the pen of an experienced sailor.

"The Try-Works" (Part III) is, of course, the bulky center of this present collection, and the pieces here are selected for literary merit and for the composite portrayal they give of Melville's masterpiece. They place *Moby-Dick* in its biographical, historical, aesthetic, and mythic perspectives.

"The Candles" (Part IV) is a cluster of shorter tributes from non-American commentators, whose appreciation is free from any charge of chauvinism, and whose angles of vision are refreshingly different.

"The Epilogue" (Part V) concludes the anthology with three floral wreaths from Herman Melville's heirs and, in a way, his poetic peers. If during the 117 years of its literary life *Moby-Dick* has suffered serious neglect, it is evident from the range in time and place of the essays in this collection that Melville's masterpiece has never completely lacked for a discerning reader, and that now his audience is legion.

H P V

Contents

1. Loomings

Anonymous, Herman Melville's Whale 2
Evert [and George?] Duyckinck, Melville's Moby Dick:
  or The Whale 5
Horace Greeley, Review of *Moby-Dick* 11
George Ripley, Review of *Moby-Dick* 14
William T. Porter [?], Moby Dick, or The Whale 17

2. The Advocate

Archibald MacMechan, The Best Sea Story Ever Written 22
Lincoln Colcord, Notes on *Moby-Dick* 32
D. H. Lawrence, Herman Melville's "Moby Dick" 44

3. The Try-Works

Henry A. Murray, In Nomine Diaboli 52
Howard C. Horsford, The Design of the Argument in *Moby-Dick* 67
Walter Bezanson, [Dynamic and Structure in *Moby-Dick*] 87
Leon Howard, The Creation of *Moby Dick* I04
Nathalia Wright, *Mosses from an Old Manse* and *Moby-Dick*:
  The Shock of Discovery 110

M. O. Percival, [Captain Ahab and Moby Dick]   116
R. W. B. Lewis, [*Moby-Dick* and Homer]   123
H. Bruce Franklin, [*Moby-Dick* as Myth]   130

4. The Candles

Emilio Cecchio, [A Note] on Melville   138
Cesare Pavese, The Literary Whaler (1923)   141
W. H. Auden, Ishmael-Melville   146
Maurius Bewley, [*Moby-Dick* and Creative Force]   152

5. Epilogue

Conrad Aiken, [*Moby-Dick* and the Puritan Dream]   160
William Faulkner, [Moby-Dick: Golgotha of the Heart]   162
Hart Crane, At Melville's Tomb   163

1. Loomings

Anonymous

Herman Melville's Whale

This sea novel is a singular medley of naval observation, magazine article writing, satiric reflection upon the conventionalisms of civilized life, and rhapsody run mad. So far as the nautical parts are appropriate and unmixed, the portraiture is truthful and interesting. Some of the satire, especially in the early parts, is biting and reckless. The chapter-spinning is various in character; now powerful from the vigorous and fertile fancy of the author, now little more than empty though sounding phrases. The rhapsody belongs to wordmongering where ideas are the staple; where it takes the shape of narrative or dramatic fiction, it is phantasmal — an attempted description of what is impossible in nature and without probability in art; it repels the reader instead of attracting him.

The elements of the story are a South Sea whaling voyage, narrated by Ishmael, one of the crew of the ship Pequod, from Nantucket. Its "probable" portions consist of the usual sea matter in that branch of the industrial marine; embracing the preparations for departure, the voyage, the chase and capture of whale, with the economy of cutting up, &c., and the peculiar discipline of the

From the London *Spectator,* XXIV (October 25, 1851), 1026-1027.

service. This matter is expanded by a variety of digressions on the nature and characteristics of the sperm whale, the history of the fishery, and similar things, in which a little knowledge is made the excuse for a vast many words. The voyage is introduced by several chapters in which life in American seaports is rather broadly depicted.

The "marvellous" injures the book by disjointing the narrative, as well as by its inherent want of interest, at least as managed by Mr. Melville. In the superstition of some whalers, (grounded upon the malicious foresight which occasionally characterizes the attacks of the sperm fish upon the boats sent to capture it,) there is a *white* whale which possesses supernatural power. To capture or even to hurt it is beyond the art of man; the skill of the whaler is useless; the harpoon does not wound it; it exhibits a contemptuous strategy in its attacks upon the boats of its pursuers; and happy is the vessel where only loss of limb, or of a single life, attends its chase. Ahab, the master of the Pequod — a mariner of long experience, stern resolve, and indomitable courage, the high hero of romance, in short, transferred to a whale-ship — has lost his leg in a contest with the white whale. Instead of daunting Ahab, the loss exasperates him; and by long brooding over it his reason becomes shaken. In this condition he undertakes the voyage; making the chase of his fishy antagonist the sole object of his thoughts, and, so far as he can without exciting overt insubordination among his officers, the object of his proceedings.

Such a groundwork is hardly natural enough for a regular-built novel, though it might form a tale, if properly managed. But Mr. Melville's mysteries provoke wonder at the author rather than terror at the creation; the soliloquies and dialogues of Ahab, in which the author attempts delineating the wild imaginings of monomania, and exhibiting some profoundly speculative views of things in general, induce weariness or skipping; while the whole scheme mars, as we have said, the nautical continuity of story — greatly assisted by various chapters of a bookmaking kind. . . .

The strongest point of the book is its "characters." Ahab, indeed, is a melodramatic exaggeration, and Ishmael is little more than a mouthpiece; but the harpooners, the mates, and several of the seamen, are truthful portraitures of the sailor as modified by the whaling service. The persons ashore are equally good, though they are soon lost sight of. The two Quaker owners are the author's means for a hit at the religious hypocrisies. Captain Bildad, an old seadog, has got rid of everything pertaining to the meeting-house save an occasional "thou" and "thee." Captain Peleg, in American phrase "professes religion." . . .

It is a canon with some critics that nothing should be introduced into a novel which it is physically impossible for the writer to have known: thus, he must not describe the conversation of miners in a pit if they *all* perish. Mr. Melville hardly steers clear of this rule, and he continually violates another, by beginning in the autobiographical form and changing ad libitum into the narrative. His catastrophe overrides all rule: not only is Ahab, with his boat's-crew, destroyed in his last desperate attack upon the white whale, but the Pequod herself sinks with all on board into the depths of the illimitable ocean. Such is the go-ahead method.

Evert [and George?] Duyckinck

Melville's Moby Dick: Or, The Whale

Every reader throughout the United States has probably perused in the newspapers the account of a recent incident in the whale fishery which would stagger the mind by its extent of the marvellous, were it not paralleled by a well known case—that of the Essex of Nantucket, still authenticated by living witnesses. It appears from a narrative published in the *Panama Herald* (an American newspaper in that region, itself one of the wonders of the age!), taken down from the lips of the captain of the vessel, John S. Deblois, that the ship Ann Alexander, of New Bedford, having left that port in June of last year with the usual vicissitudes of Cape Horn service, losing a New Hampshire man overboard in a storm at that point, had entered upon her Pacific hunting-grounds, and in the recent month of August was coursing within a few degrees of the Equator—a well known haunt of the whale. On the 20th of that month, nine in the morning, fish were discovered; two boats were lowered in pursuit, and by mid-day a particular sperm whale was struck and fast to the line. The first mate commanded the boat, thus far successful, and the Captain himself the other. After

From the New York *Literary World*, IX (November 15, 1851), 381-383; (November 22, 1851), 403-404.

running some time, in the words of the narrative, the whale turned upon the boat to which he was attached, and rushing at it with tremendous violence, lifted open its enormous jaws, and taking the boat in, actually crushed it to fragments as small as a common-sized chair. Captain Deblois struck for the spot, and rescued the nine members of the boat's crew — a feat, we presume, which could only be accomplished among men hardy, resolute, and full of vitality as whalemen, strung at the moment by excitement to almost superhuman energy and superiority to the elements. The Captain, with his double boat's crew, proceeded to the ship, some six miles off. There the waist-boat was fitted out, the men divided, and both parties went again in pursuit of the whale, the mate again taking the lead. The whale perceived the coming renewal of the attack, made for the boat, crushed it with his jaw, the men again throwing themselves into the deep. The Captain once more rescuing them, was himself pursued by the whale, which passed the boat with distended jaw; but they reached the ship in safety. A boat was sent for the oars of the broken vessels floating on the water, which were secured. Sail was set on the ship, and it was determined to proceed after the whale. He was overtaken, and a lance thrown into his head! The ship passed on, when it was immediately discovered that the whale was in pursuit. The ship manœuvred out of his way. *After he had fairly passed they kept off to overtake and attack him again.* The whale settled down deep below the surface. It was then near sundown. Capt. Deblois, continues the account, was at this time standing on the knight-heads on the larboard bow, with shaft in hand, ready to strike the monster a deadly blow should he appear, the ship moving about five knots, when looking over the side of the ship he discerned the whale rushing towards her at the rate of fifteen knots. In an instant the monster struck the ship with tremendous violence, shaking her from stem to stern. She quivered under the violence of the shock as if she had struck upon a rock. Captain Deblois descending to the forecastle, discovered that *the whale had struck the ship about two feet from the keel, abreast the foremast, knocking a great hole entirely through her bottom.* The ship was sinking rapidly. All hands were ordered into the boats, the captain leaving the deck last, throwing himself into the sea, and swimming to his comrades. That night was passed in the boats, with but twelve quarts of water saved, and no provisions for twenty-two men. In the morning the ship still lay on her beam-ends. Not a man would board her to cut away the masts, right the vessel, and procure provisions — fearing her sinking instantly — except the captain, who undertook the work with a single hatchet, and succeeded in getting the ship nearly on her keel. Nothing could be procured by cutting through the decks but some vinegar and a small quantity of wet bread, with which they abandoned the dangerous vessel. At the close of the next day they hailed the ship Nantucket of Nantucket, and were welcomed by its Captain, Gibbs, with the utmost hospitality. They were landed at Paita, where an authenticated protest of this extraordinary series of occurrences was made before the United States Consul.

By a singular coincidence this extreme adventure is, even to very many of the details, the catastrophe of Mr. Melville's new book, which is a natural-historical, philosophical, romantic account of the person, habits, manners, ideas of the great sperm whale; of his haunts and of his belongings; of his associations with the world of the deep, and of the not less remarkable individuals and combinations of individuals who hunt him on the oceans. Nothing like it has ever before been written of the whale; for no man who has at once seen so much of the actual conflict, and weighed so carefully all that has been recorded on the subject, with equal powers of perception and reflection, has attempted to write at all on it—the labors of Scoresby covering a different and inferior branch of the history. To the popular mind this book of Herman Melville, touching the Leviathan of the deep, is as much of a discovery in Natural History as was the revelation of America by Christopher Columbus in geography. Let any one read this book with the attention which it deserves, and then converse with the best informed of his friends and acquaintances who have not seen it, and he will notice the extent and variety of treatment; while scientific men must admit the original observation and speculation.

Such an infuriated, resolute sperm whale as pursued and destroyed the Ann Alexander is the hero, Moby Dick, of Mr. Melville's book. The vengeance with which he is hunted, which with Capt. Deblois was the incident of a single, though most memorable day, is the leading passion and idea of Captain Ahab of the Pequod for years, and throughout the seas of the world. Incidentally with this melo-dramatic action and spiritual development of the character of Ahab, is included a full, minute, thorough investigation, and description of the whale and its fishery. Such is a short-hand account of this bulky and multifarious volume.

It opens, after a dedication to Nathaniel Hawthorne, with a preliminary flourish in the style of Carlyle and the "Doctor" of etymology, followed by a hundred or so of extracts of "Old Burton," passages of a quaint and pithy character from Job and King Alfred to Miriam Coffin; in lieu of the old style of Scott, Cooper, and others, of distributing such flourishes about the heads of chapters. Here they are all in a lump, like the grace over the Franklin barrel of pork, and may be taken as a kind of bitters, a whet and fillip to the imagination, exciting it to the curious, ludicrous, sublime traits and contemplations which are to follow. . . .

A difficulty in the estimate of this, in common with one or two other of Mr. Melville's books, occurs from the double character under which they present themselves. In one light they are romantic fictions, in another statements of absolute fact. When to this is added that the romance is made a vehicle of opinion and satire through a more or less opaque allegorical veil, as particularly in the latter half of Mardi, and to some extent in this present volume, the critical difficulty is considerably thickened. It becomes quite impossible to submit such books to a distinct classification as fact, fiction, or essay. Something of a parallel may be found in Jean Paul's German tales, with an admixture of Southey's Doctor. Under these combined influences of personal observation, actual fidelity to local truthfulness in description, a taste for reading and sentiment, a fondness for fanciful analogies, near and remote, a rash daring in speculation, reckless at times of taste and propriety, again refined and eloquent, this volume of Moby Dick may be pronounced a most remarkable sea-dish — an intellectual chowder of romance, philosophy, natural history, fine writing, good feeling, bad sayings — but over which, in spite of all uncertainties, and in spite of the author himself, predominates his keen perceptive faculties, exhibited in vivid narration.

There are evidently two if not three books in Moby Dick rolled into one. Book No. I. we could describe as a thorough exhaustive account admirably given of the great Sperm Whale. The information is minute, brilliantly illustrated, as it should be — the whale himself so generously illuminating the midnight page on which his memoirs are written — has its level pasages, its humorous touches, its quaint suggestion, its incident usually picturesque and occasionably sublime. All this is given in the most delightful manner in "The Whale." Book No. 2 is the romance of Captain Ahab, Queequeg, Tashtego, Pip & Co., who are more or less spiritual personages talking and acting differently from the general business run of the conversation on the decks of whalers. They are for the most part very serious people, and seem to be concerned a great deal about the problem of the universe. They are striking characters withal, of the romantic spiritual cast of the German drama; realities of some kinds at bottom, but veiled in all sorts of poetical incidents and expressions. As a bit of German melodrama, with Captain Ahab for the Faust of the quarter-deck, and Queequeg with the crew, for Walpurgis night revellers in the forecastle, it has its strong points, though here the limits as to space and treatment of the stage would improve it. Moby Dick in this view becomes a sort of fishy moralist, a leviathan metaphysician, a folio Ductor Dubitantium, in fact, in the fresh water illustration of Mrs. Malaprop, "an allegory on the banks of the Nile." After pursuing him in this melancholic company over a few hundred squares of latitude and longitude, we begin to have some faint idea of the association of whaling and lamentation, and why blubber is popularly synonymous with tears.

The intense Captain Ahab is too long drawn out; something more of *him* might, we think, be left to the reader's imagination. The value of this kind of writing can only be through the personal consciousness of the reader, what he brings to the book; and all this is sufficiently evoked by a dramatic trait or suggestion. If we had as much of Hamlet or Macbeth as Mr. Melville gives us of Ahab, we should be tired even of their sublime company. Yet Captain Ahab is a striking conception, firmly planted on the wild deck of the Pequod—a dark disturbed soul arraying itself with every ingenuity of material resources for a conflict at once natural and supernatural in his eye, with the most dangerous extant physical monster of the earth, embodying, in strongly drawn lines of mental association, the vaster moral evil of the world. The pursuit of the White Whale thus interweaves with the literal perils of the fishery— a problem of fate and destiny—to the tragic solution of which Ahab hurries on, amidst the wild stage scenery of the ocean. To this end the motley crew, the air, the sky, the sea, its inhabitants are idealized throughout. It is a noble and praiseworthy conception; and though our sympathies may not always accord with the train of thought, we would caution the reader against a light or hasty condemnation of this part of the work.

Book III., appropriating perhaps a fourth of the volume, is a vein of moralizing, half essay, half rhapsody, in which much refinement and subtlety, and no little poetical feeling, are mingled with quaint conceit and extravagant daring speculation. This is to be taken as in some sense dramatic; the narrator throughout among the personages of the Pequod being one Ishmael, whose wit may be allowed to be against everything on land, as his hand is against everything at sea. This piratical running down of creeds and opinions, the conceited indifferentism of Emerson, or the run-a-muck style of Carlyle is, we will not say dangerous in such cases, for there are various forces at work to meet more powerful onslaught, but it is out of place and uncomfortable. We do not like to see what, under any view, must be to the world the most sacred associations of life violated and defaced.

We call for fair play in this matter. Here is Ishmael, telling the story of this volume, going down on his knees with a cannibal to a piece of wood, in the second story fireplace of a New-Bedford tavern, in the spirit of amiable and transcendent charity, which may be all very well in its way; but why dislodge from heaven, with contumely, "long-pampered Gabriel, Michael and Raphael." Surely Ishmael, who is a scholar, might have spoken respectfully of the Archangel Gabriel, out of consideration, if not for the Bible (which might be asking too much of the school), at least for one John Milton, who wrote Paradise Lost.

Nor is it fair to inveigh against the terrors of priestcraft, which, skillful though it may be in making up its woes, at least seeks to provide a remedy for the evils of the world, and attribute the existence of conscience to "hereditary dyspepsias, nurtured by Ramadans"—and at the same time go about petrifying us with imaginary horrors, and all sorts of gloomy suggestions, all the world through. It is a curious fact that there are no more bilious people in the world, more completely filled with megrims and head shak-ings, than some of these very people who are constantly inveighing against the religious melancholy of priestcraft.

So much for the consistency of Ishmael—who, if it is the author's object to exhibit the painful contradictions of this self-dependent, self-torturing agency of a mind driven hither and thither as a flame in a whirlwind, is, in a degree, a successful embodiment of opinions, without securing from us, however, much admiration for the result.

With this we make an end of what we have been reluctantly compelled to object to this volume. With far greater pleasure, we acknowledge the acutenes of observation, the freshness of percep-tion, with which the author brings home to us from the deep, "things unattempted yet in prose or rhyme," the weird influences of his ocean scenes, the salient imagination which connects them with the past and distant, the world of books and the life of experience — certain prevalent traits of manly sentiment. These are strong powers with which Mr. Melville wrestles in this book. It would be a great glory to subdue them to the highest uses of fiction. It is still a great honor, among the crowd of successful mediocrities which throng our publishers' counters, and know nothing of devine impulses, to be in the company of these nobler spirits on any terms.

Attributed to Horace Greeley

Review of *Moby-Dick*

Everybody has heard of the tradition which is said to prevail among the old salts of Nantucket and New-Bedford, of a ferocious monster of a whale, who is proof against all the arts of harpoonery, and who occasionally amuses himself with swallowing down a boat's crew without winking. The present volume is a "Whaliad," or the Epic of that veritable old leviathan, who "esteemeth iron as straw, and laughs at the spear, the dart, and the habergeon," no one being able to "fill his skin with a barbed iron, or his head with fish-hooks." Mr. Melville gives us not only the romance of his history, but a great mass of instruction on the character and habits of his whole race, with complete details of the wily stratagems of their pursuers.

The interest of the work pivots on a certain Captain Ahab, whose enmity to Moby-Dick, the name of the whale-demon, has been aggravated to monomania. In one rencounter with this terror of the seas, he suffers a signal defeat; loses a leg in the contest; gets a fire in his brain; returns home a man with one idea; feels that he has a mission; that he is predestined to defy his enemy to mortal strife; devotes himself to the fulfillment of his destiny; with the

From the New York *Daily Tribune*, November 22, 1851.

11

persistence and cunning of insanity gets possession of another vessel; ships a weird, supernatural crew of which Ishmael, the narrator of the story, is a prominent member; and after a "wild huntsman's chase" through unknown seas, is the only one who remains to tell the destruction of the ship and the doomed Captain Ahab by the victorious, indomitable Moby-Dick.

The narrative is constructed in Herman Melville's best manner. It combines the various features which form the chief attractions of his style, and is commendably free from the faults which we have before had occasion to specify in this powerful writer. The intensity of the plot is happily relieved by minute descriptions of the most homely processes of the whale fishery. We have occasional touches of the subtle mysticism, which is carried to such an inconvenient excess in Mardi, but it is here mixed up with so many tangible and odorous realities, that we always safely alight from the excursion through mid-air upon the solid deck of the whaler. We are recalled to this world by the fumes of "oil and blubber," and are made to think more of the contents of barrels than of allegories. The work is also full of episodes, descriptive of strange and original phases of character. One of them is given in the commencement of the volume, showing how "misery makes a man acquainted with strange bed-fellows." We must pass over this in which the writer relates his first introduction to Queequeg, a South Sea cannibal, who was his chum at a sailor boarding house in New-Bedford and afterward his bosom friend and most devoted confederate. We will make a room for the characteristic chapter, which describes the ripening of their acquaintance into the honeymoon of friendship. . . .

But we must go out to sea with Ishmael, if we would witness his most remarkable exploits. We are now, then, in the midst of things, and with good luck, may soon get a sight of Moby-Dick. Meantime, we many beguile our impatience with the description of a rope on which Melville gives us a touch of his quaint moralizings. . . .

We are now ready to kill our first whale. Here is the transaction in full: "Killing a Whale." . . .

At last, Moby-Dick, the object of such long vigalant, [sic] and infuriate search, is discovered. We can only give the report of "The Chase — First Day." . . .

Here we will retire from the chase, which lasts three days, not having a fancy to be in at the death. We part with the adventurous philosophical Ishmael, truly thankful that the whale did not get his head, for which we are indebted for this wildly imaginative and truly thrilling story. We think it the best production which has yet come from that seething brain, and in spite of its lawless flights, which put all regular criticism at defiance, it gives us a higher opinion of the author's originality and power than even the favorite and fragrant first-fruits of his genius, the never-to-be-forgotten Typee.

George Ripley [?]

Review of *Moby-Dick*

A new work by Herman Melville, entitled *Moby Dick; or, The Whale*, has just been issued by Harper and Brothers, which, in point of richness and variety of incident, originality of conception, and splendor of description, surpasses any of the former productions of this highly successful author. *Moby Dick* is the name of an old White Whale; half fish and half devil; the terror of the Nantucket cruisers; the scourge of distant oceans; leading an invulnerable, charmed life; the subject of many grim and ghostly traditions. This huge sea monster has a conflict with one Captain Ahab; the veteran Nantucket salt comes off second best; not only loses a leg in the affray, but receives a twist in the brain; becomes the victim of a deep, cunning monomania; believes himself predestined to take a bloody revenge on his fearful enemy; pursues him with fierce demoniac energy of purpose; and at last perishes in the dreadful fight, just as he deems that he has reached the goal of his frantic passion. On this slight framework, the author has constructed a romance, a tragedy, and a natural history, not without numerous gratuitous suggestions on psychology, ethics, and theology. Beneath the whole

---

From Harper's *New Monthly Magazine*, IV (December, 1851), 137.

story, the subtle, imaginative reader may perhaps find a pregnant allegory, intended to illustrate the mystery of human life. Certain it is that the rapid, pointed hints which are often thrown out, with the keenness and velocity of a harpoon, penetrate deep into the heart of things, showing that the genius of the author for moral analysis is scarcely surpassed by his wizard power of description.

In the course of the narrative the habits of the whale are fully and ably described. Frequent graphic and instructive sketches of the fishery, of sea-life in a whaling vessel, and of the manners and customs of strange nations are interspersed with excellent artistic effect among the thrilling scenes of the story. The various processes of procuring oil are explained with the minute, painstaking fidelity of a statistical record, contrasting strangely with the weird, phantom-like character of the plot, and of some of the leading personages, who present a no less unearthly appearance than the witches in Macbeth. These sudden and decided transitions form a striking feature of the volume. Difficult of management, in the highest degree, they are wrought with consummate skill. To a less gifted author, they would inevitably have proved fatal. He has not only deftly avoided their dangers, but made them an element of great power. They constantly pique the attention of the reader, keeping curiosity alive, and presenting the combined charm of surprise and alternation.

The introductory chapters of the volume, containing sketches of life in the great marts of Whalingdom, New Bedford and Nantucket, are pervaded with a fine vein of comic humor, and reveal a succession of portraitures, in which the lineaments of nature shine forth, through a good deal of perverse, intentional exaggeration. To many readers, these will prove the most interesting portions of the work. Nothing can be better than the description of the owners of the vessel, Captain Peleg and Captain Bildad, whose acquaintance we make before the commencement of the voyage. The character of Captain Ahab also opens upon us with wonderful power. He exercises a wild, bewildering fascination by his dark and mysterious nature, which is not at all diminished when we obtain a clearer insight into his strange history. Indeed, all the members of the ship's company, the three mates, Starbuck, Stubbs, and Flash, the wild, savage Gayheader, the case-hardened old blacksmith, to say nothing of the pearl of a New Zealand harpooner, the bosom friend of the narrator—all stand before us in the strongest individual relief, presenting a unique picture gallery, which every artist must despair of rivaling.

The plot becomes more intense and tragic, as it approaches toward the denouement. The malicious old Moby Dick, after long cruisings in pursuit of him, is at length discovered. He comes up to the battle, like an army with banners. He seems inspired with the same fierce, inveterate cunning with which Captain Ahab has followed the traces of his mortal foe. The fight is described in letters of blood. It is easy to foresee which will be the victor in such a contest. We need not say that the ill-omened ship is broken in fragments by the wrath of the weltering fiend. Captain Ahab becomes the prey of his intended victim. The crew perish. One alone escapes to tell the tale. Moby Dick disappears unscathed, and for aught we know, is the same "delicate monster," whose power in destroying another ship is just announced from Panama.

William T. Porter [?]

Moby Dick, or The Whale

Our friend Melville's books begin to accumulate. His literary family increases rapidly. He had already a happy and smiling progeny around him, but lo! at the appointed time another child of his brain, with the accustomed signs of the family, claims our attention and regard. We bid the book a hearty welcome. We assure the "happy father" that his "labors of love" are no "love's labor lost."

We confess an admiration for Mr. Melville's books, which, perhaps, spoils us for mere criticism. There are few writers, living or dead, who describe the sea and its adjuncts with such true art, such graphic power, and with such powerfully resulting interest. "Typee," "Omoo," "Redburn," "Mardi," and "White Jacket," are equal to anything in the language. They are things of their own. They are results of the youthful experience on the ocean of a man who is at once philosopher, painter, and poet. This is not, perhaps, a very unusual mental combination, but it is not usual to find such a combination "before the mast." So far Mr. Melville's early experiences, though perhaps none of the pleasantest to himself,

From the New York *Spirit of the Times*, XXI (December 6, 1851).

17

are infinitely valuable to the world. We say *valuable* with a full knowleldge of the terms used; and, not to enter into details, which will be fresh in the memory of most of Mr. Melville's readers, it is sufficient to say that the humanities of the world have been quickened by his works. Who can forget the missionary *expose*—the practical good sense which pleads for "Poor Jack," or the unsparing but just severity of his delineations of naval abuses, and that crowning disgrace to our navy—flogging? Taken as matters of art these books are amongst the largest and the freshest contributions of original thought and observation which have been presented in many years. Take the majority of modern writers, and it will be admitted that however much they may elaborate and rearrange the stock of ideas pre-existant, there is little added to this "common fund." Philosophers bark at each other—poets sing stereotyped phrases—John Miltons re-appear in innumerable "Pollock's Courses of Time"—novelists and romances stick to the same overdone incidents, careless of the memories of defunct Scotts and Radcliffs, and it is only now and then when genius, by some lucky chance of youth, ploughs deeper into the soil of humanity and nature, that fresher experience—perhaps at the cost of much individual pain and sorrow—are obtained; and the results are books, such as those of Herman Melville and Charles Dickens. Books which are living pictures, at once of the practical truth, and the ideal amendment: books which mark epochs in literature and art.

It is, however, not with Mr. Melville generally as a writer that we have now to deal, but with "Moby Dick, or the Whale," in particular; and at first let us not forget to say that in "taking titles" no man is more felicitous than our author. Sufficiently dreamy to excite one's curiosity, sufficiently explicit to indicate some main and peculiar feature. "Moby Dick" is perhaps a creation of the brain—"The Whale" a result of experience; and the whole title a fine polished result of both. A title may be a truth or a lie. It may be clap-trap, or true art. A bad book may have a good title, but you will seldom find a good book with an inappropriate name.

•   •   •

"Moby Dick, or the Whale," is all whale. Leviathan is here in full amplitude. Not one of your museum affairs, but the real, living whale, a bona-fide, warm-blooded creature, ransacking the waters

from pole to pole. His enormous bulk, his terribly destructive
energies, his habits, his food, are all before us. Nay, even his lighter
moods are exhibited. We are permitted to see the whale as a lover,
a husband, and the head of a family. So to speak, we are made
guests at his fire-side; we set our mental legs beneath his mahogany,
and become members of his interesting social circle. No book in the
world brings together so much whale. We have his history, natural
and social, living and dead. But Leviathan's natural history, though
undoubtedly valuable to science, is but a part of the book. It is in
the personal adventures of his captors, their toils, and, alas! not
unfrequently their wounds and martyrdom, that our highest interest
is excited. This mingling of human adventure with new, startling,
and striking objects and pursuits, constitute one of the chief charms
of Mr. Melville's books. His present work is a drama of intense
interest. A whale, "Moby Dick" — a dim, gigantic, unconquerable,
but terribly destructive being, is one of the persons of the drama.
We admit a disposition to be critical on this character. We had
doubts as to his admissibility as an actor into dramatic action, and
so it would seem had our author, but his chapter, "The Affidavit,"
disarms us; all improbability or incongruity disappears, and "Moby
Dick" becomes a living fact, simply doubtful at first, because he
was so new an idea, one of those beings whose whole life, like the
Palladius or the Sea-serpent, is a romance, and whose memoirs
unvarnished are of themselves a fortune to the first analist or his
publisher.

"Moby Dick, or the Whale," is a "many-sided" book. Mingled
with much curious information respecting whales and whaling there
is a fine vein of sermonizing, a good deal of keen satire, much
humor, and that too of the finest order, and a story of peculiar
interest. As a romance its characters are so new and unusual that
we doubt not it will excite the ire of critics. It is not tame enough
to pass this ordeal safely. Think of a monomaniac whaling captain,
who, mutilated on a former voyage by a particular whale, well
known for its peculiar bulk, shape, and color — seeks, at the risk
of his life and the lives of his crew, to capture and slay this terror
of the seas! It is on this idea that the romance hinges. The usual
staple of novelists is entirely wanting. We have neither flinty-
hearted fathers, designing villains, dark caverns, men in armor, nor
anxious lovers. There is not in the book any individual, who, at a
certain hour, *"might have been seen"* ascending hills or descending
valleys, as is usual. The thing is entirely new, fresh, often startling,

and highly dramatic, and with those even, who, oblivious of other fine matters, scattered with profusest hand, read for the sake of the story, must be exceedingly successful.

• • •

Did our limits permit we would gladly extract the fine little episode, contained in the chapter called "The Castaway," as a favorable specimen of Mr. Melville's graphic powers of description. But we must conclude by strongly recommending "Moby Dick, or the Whale," to all who can appreciate a work of exceeding power, beauty, and genius.

2. The Advocate

Archibald MacMechan

The Best Sea Story
Ever Written

Any one who undertakes to reverse some judgment in history or criticism, or to set the public right regarding some neglected man or work, becomes at once an object of suspicion. Nine times out of ten he is called a literary snob for his pains, or a prig who presumes to teach his betters, or a "phrase-monger," or a "young Osric," or something equally soul-subduing. Besides, the burden of proof lies heavy upon him. He preaches to a sleeping congregation. The good public has returned its verdict upon the case, and is slow to review the evidence in favour of the accused, or, having done so, to confess itself in the wrong. Still, difficult as the work of rehabilitation always is, there are cheering instances of its complete success; notably, the rescue of the Elizabethan dramatists by Lamb and Hazlitt and Leight Hunt. Nor in such a matter is the will always free. As Heine says, ideas take possession of us and force us into the arena, there to fight for them. There is also the possibility of triumph to steel the raw recruit against all dangers. Though the world at large may not care, the judicious few may be glad of new light, and may feel satisfaction in seeing even tardy justice meted out to real merit.

From *Queen's Quarterly*, VII (October, 1899), 181-197.

In my poor opinion much less than justice has been done to an American writer, whose achievement is so considerable that it is hard to account for the neglect into which he has fallen.

This writer is Herman Melville, who died in New York in the autumn of 1891, aged eighty-three. That his death excited little attention is in consonance with the popular apathy towards him and his work. The civil war marks a dividing line in his literary production as well as in his life. His best work belongs to the *ante-bellum* days, and is cut off in taste and sympathy from the distinctive literary fashions of the present time. To find how complete neglect is, one has only to put question to the most cultivated and patriotic Americans north or south, east or west, even professed specialists in the nativist literature, and it will be long before the Melville enthusiast meets either sympathy or understanding. The present writer made his first acquaintance with *Moby Dick* in the dim, dusty Mechanics' Institute Library (opened once a week by the old doctor) or an obscure Canadian village, nearly twenty years ago; and since that time he has seen only one copy of the book exposed for sale, and met only one person (and that not an American) who had read it. Though Kingsley has a good word for Melville, the only place where real appreciation of him is to be found of recent years is in one of Mr. Clark Russell's dedications. There occurs the phrase which gives this paper its title. Whoever takes the trouble to read this unique and original book will concede that Mr. Russell knows whereof he affirms.

Melville is a man of one book, and this fact accounts possibly for much of his unpopularity. The marked inferiority of his work after the war, as well as changes in literary fashion, would drag the rest down with it. Nor are his earliest works, embodying personal experience like *Redburn* and *White Jacket,* quite worthy of the pen which wrote *Moby Dick. Omoo* and *Typee* are little more than sketches, legitimately idealized, of his own adventures in the Marquesas. They are notable works in that they are the first to reveal to civilized people the charm of life in the islands of the Pacific, the charm which is so potent in *Vailima Letters* and *The Beach of Falesà.* Again, the boundless archipelagos of Oceanica furnish the scenes of *Mardi,* his curious political satire. This contains a prophecy of the war, and a fine example of obsolete oratory in the speech of the great chief Alanno from Hio-Hio. The prologue in a whale-ship and the voyage in an open boat are, perhaps, the most interesting parts. None of his books are without distinct and peculiar excellences, but nearly all have some fatal fault. Melville's seems a case of arrested literary development. The power and promise of power in his best work are almost unbounded; but he either did not care to follow them up or he had worked out all his rifts of ore. The last years of his life he spent as a recluse.

His life fitted him to write his one book. The representative of a good old Scottish name, his portrait shows distinctively Scottish traits. The head is the sort that goes naturally with a tall, powerful figure. The forehead is broad and square; the hair is abundant; the full beard masks the mouth and chin; the general aspect is of great but disciplined strength. The eyes are level and determined; they have speculation in them. Nor does his work belie his blood. It shows the natural bent of the Scot towards metaphysics; and this thoughtfulness is one pervading quality of Melville's books. In the second place, his family had been so long established in the country (his grandfather was a member of the "Boston tea-party") that he secured the benefits of education and inherited culture: and this enlightenment was indispensable in enabling him to perceive the literary "values" of the strange men, strange scenes and strange events amongst which he was thrown. And then, he had the love of adventure which drove him forth to gather his material at the ends of the earth. He made two voyages; first as a green hand of eighteen in one of the old clipper packets to Liverpool and back; and next, as a young man of twenty-three, in a whaler. The latter was sufficiently adventurous. Wearying of sea-life, he deserted on one of the Marquesas Islands, and came near being killed and eaten by cannibal natives who kept him prisoner for four months. At last he escaped, and worked his way home on a U.S. man-o'-war. This adventure lasted four years and he went no more to sea.

After his marriage, he lived at Pittsfield for thirteen years, in close intimacy with Hawthorne, to whom he dedicated his chief work. My copy shows that it was written as early as 1851, but the title page is dated exactly twenty years later. It shows as its three chief elements this Scottish thoughtfulness, the love of literature and the love of adventure.

When Mr. Clark Russell singles out *Moby Dick* for such high praise as he bestows upon it, we think at once of other sea-stories, —his own, Marryatt's, Smollet's perhaps, and such books as Dana's *Two Years before the Mast*. But the last is a plain record of fact; in Smollet's tales, sea-life is only part of one great round of adventure; in Mr. Russell's mercantile marine, there is generally the romantic interest of the way of a man with a maid; and in Marryatt's the rise of a naval officer through various ranks plus a love-story or plenty of fun, fighting and prize-money. From all these advantages Melville not only cuts himself off, but seems to heap all sorts of obstacles in his self appointed path. Great are the prejudices to be overcome; but he triumphs over all. Whalers are commonly regarded as a sort of sea-scavengers. He convinces you that their business is poetic; and that they are finest fellows afloat. He dispenses with a love-story altogether; there is hardly a flutter of a petticoat from chapter first to last. The book is not a record of fact; but of fact idealized, which supplies the frame for a terrible duel to the death between a mad whaling-captain and a miraculous white sperm whale. It is not a love-story but a story of undying hate.

In no other tale is one so completely detached from the land, even from the very suggestion of land. Though Nantucket and New Bedford must be mentioned, only their nautical aspects are touched on; they are but the steps of the saddle-block from which the mariner vaults upon the back of his sea-horse. The strange ship "Pequod" is the theatre of all the strange adventures. For ever off soundings, she shows but as a central speck in a wide circle of blue or stormy sea; and yet a speck crammed full of human passions, the world itself in little. Comparison brings out only the more strongly the unique character of the book. Whaling is the most peculiar business done by man upon the deep waters. A war-ship is but a mobile fort or battery; a merchantman is but a floating shop or warehouse: fishing is devoid of any but the ordinary perils of navigation; but sperm-whaling, according to Melville, is the most exciting and dangerous kind of big game hunting. One part of the author's triumph consists in having made the complicated operations of this strange pursuit perfectly familiar to the reader; and that not in any dull, pedantic fashion, but touched with the imagination, the humor, the fancy, the reflection of a poet. His intimate knowledge of his subject and his intense interest in it make the whaler's life in all its details not only comprehensible but fascinating.

A bare outline of the story, though it cannot suggest its peculiar charm, may arouse a desire to know more about it. The book takes its name from a monstrous, invincible, sperm whale of diabolical strength and malice. In an encounter with this leviathan, Ahab, the captain of a Nantucket whaler, has had his leg torn off. The long illness which ensues drives him mad; and his one thought upon recovery is vengeance upon the creature that has mutilated him. He gets command of the "Pequod," concealing his purpose with the cunning of insanity until the fitting moment comes: then he swears the whole crew into his fatal vendetta. From this point on, the mad captain bears down all opposition, imposes his own iron will upon the ship's company, and affects them with like heat, until they are as one keen weapon fitted to his hand and to his purpose. In spite of all difficulties, in spite of all signs and portents and warnings, human and divine, he drives on to certain destruction. Everything conduces to one end, a three day's battle with the monster, which staves and sinks the ship, like the ill-fated "Essex."

For a tale of such length, *Moby Dick* is undoubtedly well constructed. Possibly the "Town-Ho's Story," interesting as it is, somewhat checks the progress of the plot; but by the time the reader reaches this point, he is infected with the leisurely, trade-wind, whaling atmosphere, and has no desire to proceed faster than at the "Pequod's" own cruising rate. Possibly the book might be shortened by excision, but when one looks over the chapters it is hard to decide which to sacrifice. The interest begins with the quaint words of the opening sentence: "Call me Ishmael"; and never slackens for at least a hundred pages. Ishmael's reasons for going to sea, his sudden friendship with Queequeg, the Fijian harpooner, Father Mapple's sermon on Jonah, in the seamen's bethel, Queequeg's rescue of the country bumpkin on the way to Nantucket, Queequeg's Ramadan, the description of the ship "Pequod" and her two owners, Elijah's warning, getting under way and dropping the pilot, make up an introduction of great variety and picturesqueness. The second part deals with all the particulars of the various operations in whaling from manning the mast-heads and lowering the boats to trying out the blubber and cleaning up the ship, when all the oil is barrelled. In this part Ahab, who has been invisible in the retirement of his cabin, comes on deck and in various scenes different sides of his vehement, iron-willed, yet pathetic nature, are made intelligible. Here also is much learning to be found, and here, if anywhere, the story dawdles. The last part deals with the fatal three days' chase, the death of Ahab, and the escape of the White Whale.

One striking peculiarity of the book is its Americanism — a word which needs definition. The theme and style are peculiar to this country. Nowhere but in America could such a theme have been treated in such a style. Whaling is peculiarly an American industry; and of all whale men, the Nantucketers were the keenest, the most daring, and the most successful. Now, though there are still whalers to be found in the New Bedford slips, and interesting as it is to clamber about them and hear the unconscious confirmation of all Melville's details from the lips of some old harpooner or boat-header, the industry is almost extinct. The discovery of petroleum did for it. Perhaps Melville went to sea for no other purpose than to construct the monument of whaling in this unique book. Not in his subject alone, but in his style is Melville distinctly American. It is large in idea, expansive; it has an Elizabethan force and freshness and swing, and is, perhaps, more rich in figures than any style but Emerson's. It has the picturesqueness of the new world, and, above all, a free-flowing humour, which is the distinct *cachet* of American literature. No one would contend that it is a perfect style; some mannerisms become tedious, like the constant moral turn, and the curiously coined adverbs placed before the verb. Occasionally there is more than a hint of bombast, as indeed might be expected; but, upon the whole, it is an extraordinary style, rich, clear, vivid, original. It shows reading and is full of thought and allusion; but its chief charm is its freedom from all scholastic rules and conventions. Melville is a Walt Whitman of prose.

Like Browning he has a dialect of his own. The poet of *The Ring and the Book* translates the different emotions and thoughts and possible words of pope, jurist, murderer, victim, into one level uniform Browningese; reduces them to a common denominator, in a way of speaking, and Melville gives us not the actual words of American whalemen, but what they would say under the imagined conditions, translated into one consistent, though various Melvillesque manner of speech. The life he deals with belongs already to the legendary past, and he has us completely at his mercy. He is completely successful in creating his "atmosphere." Granted the conditions, the men and their words, emotions and actions, all are consistent. One powerful scene takes place on the quarter-deck of the "Pequod" one evening, when, all hands mustered aft, the Captain Ahab tells of the White Whale, and offers a doubloon to the first man who "raises" him:

> " 'Captain Ahab,' said Tashtego, 'that White Whale must be the same that some call Moby Dick.'
> 'Moby Dick?' shouted Ahab. 'Do ye know the white whale then Tash?'
> 'Does he fan-tail a little curious, sir, before he goes down?' said the Gay-Header, deliberately.
> 'And has he a curious spout, too,' said Daggoo, 'very bushy, even for a parmacetty, and mighty quick, Captain Ahab?'

'And he have one, two, tree—oh good many iron in him hide, too, Captain,' cried Queequeg, disjointedly, 'all twisktee be-twisk, like him—him—' faltering hard for a word, and screwing his hand round and round as though uncorking a bottle—'like him—him—'

'Corkscrew!' cried Ahab, 'aye, Queequeg, the harpoons lie all twisted and wrenched in him; aye, Daggoo, his spout is a big one, like a whole shock of wheat, and white as a pile of our Nantucket wool after the great annual sheep-shearing; aye, Tashtego, *and he fan-tails like a split jib in a squall.*'

The first mate, Starbuck, asks him, 'it was not Moby Dick that took off thy leg?'

'Who told thee that?' cried Ahab; then pausing, 'Aye, Starbuck; aye, my hearties all round, it was Moby Dick that dismasted me Moby Dick that brought me to this dead stump I stand on now. Aye, aye,' he shouted with a terrific, loud, animal sob, like that of a heart-stricken moose; 'Aye, aye! it was that accursed white whale that razeed me; made a poor pegging lubber of me for ever and a day!'

Starbuck alone attempts to withstand him.

'Vengeance on a dumb brute!' cried Starbuck, 'that simply smote thee from the blindest instinct! Madness; to be enraged with a dumb thing, Captain Ahab, seems blasphemous.'

'Hark ye, yet again,—the little lower layer. All visible objects, man, are but as pasteboard masks. But in each event—in the living act, the undoubted deed—there, some unknown but still reasoning thing puts forth the mouldings of its features from behind the unreasoning mask. If man will strike, strike through the mask!' "

Then follows the wild ceremony of drinking round the capstan-head from the harpoon-sockets to confirm Ahab's curse. "Death to Moby Dick. God hunt us all, if we do not hunt Moby Dick to the death!" The intermezzo of the various sailors on the forecastle which follows until the squall strikes the ship is one of the most suggestive passages in all the literature of the sea. Under the influence of Ahab's can, the men are dancing on the forecastle. The old Manx sailor says:

"I wonder whether those jolly lads bethink them of what they are dancing over. I'll dance over your grave, I will—that's the bitterest threat of your night-women, that beat head-winds round corners. O, Christ! to think of the green navies and the green-skulled crews."

Where every page, almost every paragraph, has its quaint or telling phrase, or thought, or suggested picture, it is hard to make a selection; and even the choicest morsels give you no idea of the richness of the feast. Melville's humour has been mentioned; it is a constant quantity. Perhaps the statement of his determination after the adventure of the first lowering is as good an example as any:

> "Here, then, from three impartial witnesses, I had a deliberate statement of the case. Considering, therefore, that squalls and capsizings in the water, and consequent bivouacks in the deep, were matters of common occurrence in this kind of life; considering that at the superlatively critical moment of going on to the whale I must resign my life into the hands of him who steered the boat — oftentimes a fellow who at that very moment is in his impetuousness upon the point of scuttling the craft with his own frantic stampings; considering that the particular disaster to our own particular boat was chiefly to be imputed to Starbuck's driving on to his whale, almost in the teeth of a squall, and considering that Starbuck, notwithstanding, was famous for his great heedfulness in the fishery; considering that I belonged to this uncommonly prudent Starbuck's boat; and finally considering in what a devil's chase I was implicated, touching the White Whale: taking all things together, I say, I thought I might as well go below and make a rough draft of my will.
>
> 'Queequeg,' said I, 'come along and you shall be my lawyer, executor and legatee.' "

The humor has the usual tinge of Northern melancholy, and sometimes a touch of Rabelais. The exhortations of Stubb to his boat's crew, on different occasions, or such chapters as "Queen Mab," "The Cassock," "Leg and Arm," "Stubb's Supper," are good examples of his peculiar style.

But, after all, his chief excellence is bringing to the landsman the very salt of the sea breeze, while to one who has long known the ocean, he is as one praising to the lover the chiefest beauties of the Beloved. The magic of the ship and the mystery of the sea are put into words that form pictures for the dullest eyes. The chapter, "The Spirit Spout," contains these two aquarelles of the moonlit sea and the speeding ship side by side:

> "It was while gliding through these latter waters that one serene and moonlight night, when all the waves rolled by like scrolls of silver; and by their soft, suffusing seethings all things made what seemed a silvery silence, not a solitude; on such a silent night a silvery jet was seen far in advance of the white bubbles at the bow. Lit up by the moon it looked celestial; seemed some plumed and glittering god uprising from the sea.   *   *   *   *   *

Walking the deck, with quick, side-lunging strides, Ahab commanded the t'gallant sails and royals to be set, and every stunsail
spread. The best man in the ship must take the helm. Then, with
every mast-head manned, the piled-up craft rolled down before the
wind. The strange, upheaving, lifting tendency of the taffrail breeze
filling the hollows of so many sails made the buoyant, hovering deck
to feel like air beneath the feet."

In the chapter called "The Needle," ship and sea and sky are
blended in one unforgettable whole:

"Next morning the not-yet-subsided sea rolled in long, slow bil-
lows of mighty bulk, and striving in the "Pequod's" gurgling track,
pushed her on like giants' palms outspread. The strong, unstagger-
ing breeze abounded so, that sky and air seemed vast outbellying
sails; the whole world boomed before the wind. Muffled in the full
morning light, the invisible sun was only known by the spread intensity of his place; where his bayonet rays moved on in stacks.
Emblazonings, as of crowned Babylonian kings and queens, reigned
over everything. The sea was a crucible of molten gold, that bub-
blingly leaps with light and heat."

It would be hard to find five consecutive sentences anywhere
containing such pictures and such vivid, pregnant, bold imagery:
but this book is made up of such things.

The hero of the book is, after all, not Captain Ahab, but his triumphant antagonist, the mystic white monster of the sea, and it is
only fitting that he should come for a moment at least into the
saga. A complete scientific memoir of the Sperm Whale as known
to man might be quarried from this book, for Melville has described
the creature from his birth to his death, and even burial in the oil
casks and the ocean. He has described him living, dead and anato-
mized. At least one such description is in place here. The appearance of the whale on the second day of the fatal chase is by
"breaching," and nothing can be clearer than Melville's account
of it:

"The triumphant halloo of thirty buckskin lungs was heard, as—
much nearer to the ship than the place of the imaginary jet, less than
a mile ahead—Moby Dick bodily burst into view! For not by any
calm and indolent spoutings; not by the peaceable gush of that
mystic fountain in his head, did the White Whale now reveal his
vicinity; but by the far more wondrous phenomenon of breaching.
Rising with his utmost velocity from the furthest depths, the Sperm

Whale thus booms his entire bulk into the pure element of air, and
piling up a mountain of dazzling foam, shows his place to the distance of seven miles and more. In those moments the torn, enraged
waves he shakes off seem his mane; in some cases this breaching is
his act of defiance.

'There she breaches! there she breaches!' was the cry, as in his
immeasurable bravadoes the White Whale tossed himself salmon-
like to heaven. So suddenly seen in the blue plain of the sea, and
relieved against the still bluer margin of the sky, the spray that he
raised for the moment intolerably glittered and glared like a glacier;
and stood there gradually fading and fading away from its first
sparkling intensity to the dim mistiness of an advancing shower in
a vale."

This book is at once the epic and the encyclopaedia of whaling.
It is a monument to the honour of an extinct race of daring seamen;
but it is a monument overgrown with the lichen of neglect. Those
who will care to scrape away the moss may be few, but they will
have their reward. To the class of gentleman-adventurer, to those
who love both books and free life under the wide and open sky, it
must always appeal. Melville takes rank with Borrow, and Jefferies,
and Thoreau, and Sir Richard Burton; and his place in this brother-
hood of notables is not the lowest. Those who feel the salt in their
blood that draws them time and again out of the city to the
wharves and the ships, almost without their knowledge or their
will; those who feel the irresistible lure of the spring, away from
the cramped and noisy town, up the long road to the peaceful companionship of the awakening earth and the untainted sky; all those
— and they are many — will find in Melville's great book an ever
fresh and constant charm.

Lincoln Colcord

Notes on *Moby-Dick*

Fresh from a second reading of Melville's "Moby Dick," I am surprised by the heterodoxy of certain strong impressions. It is a book which leads to violent convictions. I first read it as a boy, on shipboard, somewhere about the world; I was enthralled by the story, but beyond a keen sensation of pleasure I retained no definite recollection of it. Thus, upon a second reading, the book had for me all the delight of a new discovery. Again I was enthralled, this time by more than the story; by all the infernal power and movement of the piece, by that intangible quality which, through suggestion and stimulation, gives off the very essence of genius. I do not mean atmosphere—Conrad creates atmosphere—but something above atmosphere, the aura of sublime and tragic greatness; not light but illumination, the glance of a brooding and unappeasable god.

The art of "Moby Dick" as a masterpiece of fiction lies in the element of purposeful suspense which flows through the tale from beginning to end in a constantly swelling current; and in the ac-

From *The Freeman*, V (August 23 and 30, 1922), 559-562, 585-587.

cumulating grandeur and terror evoked by the whale-*motif*. This achievement which, like every such feat of genius, defies either description or criticism, is what makes the book superlatively great. Melville performs the most difficult task of literary creation—that of encompassing and fixing the vague form of a tremendous visionary conception.

The high-water mark of inspiration in the book is reached in the dramatic dialogue between Ahab and the carpenter over the making of the wooden leg. This scene is preceded by the finest piece of descriptive characterization in the volume, written in Melville's own style (not aped after Sir Thomas Browne) : the sketch of the old ship-carpenter. Starting abruptly from the heights of this description, the dialogue soars straight to the realm of pure literary art. It is the equal of Shakespeare's best dialogue. One longs to hear it given by a couple of capable actors: the scene, the confusion of the "Pequod's" deck by night on the whaling-grounds; the lurid flame of the smithy in the background, in the foreground the old bewhiskered carpenter planing away at Ahab's ivory leg; before the footlights an audience familiar with the book, or, lacking this, any intelligent audience, the want of special knowledge being supplied by a plain prologue. The scene exactly as it stands is magnificently dramatic.

This, however, is a burst of inspiration. The ablest piece of sustained writing in "Moby Dick" unquestionably is the extraordinary chapter on "The Whiteness of the Whale." Here we have a *tour de force* without excuse in the narrative, a mere joyous rush of exhilaration and power, a throwing out of the arms with a laugh and a flash of the eye. "The Whiteness of the Whale," I said to myself, as I came to this chapter; "what the devil have we now?" I feared that Melville would exceed his licence, that he might be going to strain the case a little. For it seemed an inconsequential heading for a chapter; and when I ran over the leaves, noting how long the effort was, my heart misgave me. But before a page is finished, the reader catches the idea and perceives the masterliness of the attack. Throughout the chapter, as one watches the author play with his theme, letting it rise and fall naturally (nothing is ever still that comes from Melville's hand — even his calms shimmer and shake with an intensity of heat); as one follows this magically dexterous exercise, all of which, apart from its intrinsic beauty, contributes in some ineffable manner to the charm and mystery of the tale; one is aware of the thrill which comes but seldom in a lifetime of reading.

As a piece of sheer writing, this chapter on the whiteness of the whale is a remarkable achievement. Its creator could do anything with words. I wonder that it has not been more commonly utilized in the higher teaching of English; I know of no effort in the language which affords a better study of what can be accomplished by the magic of literary power.

II

"Moby Dick" stands as one of the great nautical books of the world's literature. What I have to say of it on this score, therefore, may to Melville's public, which is almost exclusively a shore-public, appear to be malicious heresy. But I am concerned only with establishing what seems to me an interesting verity; I want to find the real Melville, because he is so well worth finding; I would not be engaged in criticism had I not first become engaged in love and admiration.

I am surprised, when all is said and done, to find how little of real nautical substance there is in "Moby Dick." It would not be overstating the case to say that the book lacks the final touch of nautical verisimilitude. In criticizing the book from this viewpoint, one must, of course, make due allowance for the refining and rarifying influence of the imaginative pitch to which the whole work is cast; an influence which naturally tends to destroy a share of nautical realism, as, indeed, it tends to destroy all realism. Yet, when this allowance is made, there remains in "Moby Dick" a certain void, difficult of estimate or description, where the shadows, at least, of nautical reality should stand.

This void, of course, appears only to the sailor who reads the book; no one else would notice it. It is not that the book lacks the framework of nautical reality; it would be idle for me to attempt to deny what plainly exists. "Moby Dick," indeed, is in the generic sense of the term a nautical piece; it is a tale of ships, sailing, and the sea. We have a view of the "Pequod," of certain seafaring scenes and operations; we have a picture of the business of whaling, the handling of boats, the cutting in of the great fish alongside the ship, the final labours on deck and in the hold; we have a general background of nautical affairs, so that the scenes inevitably stand out against a tracery of sails, clouds, horizon and sea; and all this is correctly written, from the nautical standpoint, save in a few insignificant particulars. Melville's treatment of the whaling-industry, in fact, is classic. No one else has done such work, and no one ever will do it again; it alone serves to rescue from oblivion one of the most extraordinary episodes of human enterprise.

But this fidelity to the business of whaling is not precisely what I mean by nautical verisimilitude. How, then, shall I define the lack of this verisimilitude which I find in "Moby Dick"? Shall I put it that there is not quite enough of sure detail, in any instance where a nautical scene or evolution is described, to convince the sailor-reader that the man who wrote the words understood with full instinctive knowledge what he was writing about? A sailor, a seaman in the real sense of the word, would involuntarily have followed so closely the scene or evolution in hand, that he could not have fallen short of the final touch óf realism; he would himself have been a part of the picture, he would quite unconsciously have written from that point of view, and the added colour and particularity, in the case of "Moby Dick," far from detracting from the strength and purpose of the work, would on the contrary have considerably augmented them.

Melville, quite unconsciously, did not write the book that way. To his eye, indeed, it plainly was not so much a nautical work as it was a study in the boundless realm of human psychology. Yet, having taken the sea for his background, he could not have failed, had he been a sailor, to fill the void I mention. From this one gets a measure of Melville's spiritual relation to seafaring.

Most mysteries submit to a simple explanation; they are no mysteries at all. In the present case, a closer view of seafaring alone is needed. All Melville's seafaring experience lay before the mast. He gives no indication that he was in the least degree interested in this experience as a romantic profession; he speaks of obeying orders, admitting that those who command his activities on the sea had a right to require him to do anything under the sun; but I have never seen a passage in which he celebrated the task of learning to be a good seaman—except as a piece of extraneous description—or one showing the slightest interest in the sea professionally. He was decidedly not looking towards the quarter-deck. When afloat, he seems simply to have ben mooning around the vessel, indulging his fancy to the full, chiefly observing human nature; realistically intent on the ship's company, but merely romanticizing over the ship herself; in short, not making any advance towards becoming himself a sailor, towards the acquisition of those instinctive reactions which make man and ship dual parts of the same entity.

I would not be thought so absurd as to blame Melville for not becoming a true sailor; I am merely trying to run the fact to earth.

He was divinely inefficient as a seaman; he never learned the lore of a ship, beyond attaining the necessary familiarity with her external parts, with the execution of simple commands, and with the broader features of her control and operation. His nautical psychology was that of the forecastle, the psychology of obeying orders. For months on end, at sea, he felt no curiosity to know where the ship was or whither she was going; he never understood exactly why she was made to perform certain evolutions; he helped to execute the order, and watched the result with a mild and romantic perplexity. The psychology of the quarter-deck, the psychology of handling a vessel, was foreign to him.

This is why his nautical atmosphere is made up of relatively unimportant details and insignificant evolutions, such as a green man before the mast would have compassed; while infinitely more important details and more significant evolutions, and the grasp of the whole ship as a reality, all of which would have been in the direct line of the narrative, and would only have intensified the effect he was striving to produce, were passed over in silence because they were beyond his ken. He might have made the ship, as well as the whale, contribute to the mysterious grandeur of the book's main theme; in no single instance does he attempt to do so. The "Pequod," to all intents and purposes, is a toy ship; when, indeed, she is not a ship nautically fictitious, a land-lubber's ship, a ship doing the impossible.

If Captain Ahab says "Brace the yards!" once, he says it a hundred times; whereas there are dozens of commands that he might have shouted with stronger effect, both realistic and literary; whereas, furthermore, the order to "brace the yards" means nothing in particular, without a qualifying direction, and never would be given in this incomplete form on a ship's deck. This is a minor instance; but the sum of these nautical ineptitudes throughout the book is fairly staggering.

To cite a major instance, the account of the typhoon off the coast of Japan is a sad failure; it might have been written by one of your Parisian arm-chair romanticists, with a knowledge of the sea derived from a bathing-beach experience. The ship is an imaginary piece of mechanism; no coherent sense of the storm itself is created; no realization of the behaviour of a vessel in a typhoon runs behind the pen. Ahab's battered quadrant, thrown to the deck and trampled on the day before, is allowed to come through the storm reposing as it fell, so that his eye may be caught by it there when the weather has cleared. In fact, both as a piece of writing and as an essential of the tale, the scene wholly fails to justify itself. It serves no apparent purpose; it seems to have been lugged in by the ears.

How a man with an experience of some years on the sea, a man who could write the superlative chapter on the whiteness of the whale, should fail so completely to present an adequate or even an understanding picture of a ship beset by a heavy circular storm — here is a mystery not so easy of solution. It would seem to be plainly evident that Melville had never passed through a typhoon, and never, probably, had been on the Japan whaling-grounds. But he must have seen plenty of storms at sea. With all his passionate descriptive power, however, he is strangely handicapped when he comes to imagine a scene beyond the range of his experience; his literary equipment did not readily lend itself to the translation of an imaginative picture in terms of reality.

Certainly Melville had in his blood none of the "feeling of the sea," that subtle reaction which is the secret animating spring of the real sailor. Romantic appreciation he had, and imaginative sentiment; but these must never be confounded with seamanship. Yet, in defence of his nautical laxity in the latter half of "Moby Dick," it should be recognized that, by the time he had reached these chapters, he must have been exhausted with the intensity of the emotional effort; and that, after juggling with forms for two-thirds of the volume, he had now definitely forsaken all attempts at realism. Ahab alone would have worn out an ordinary man in short order.

III

I do not remember having seen in print a discussion of the extraordinary technical development of "Moby Dick." In terms of the craft of writing, the book is a surpassing feat of legerdemain. Briefly, "Moby Dick" is the only piece of fiction I know of, which at one and the same time is written in the first and the third persons. It opens straightforwardly as first-person narration. "Call me Ishmael" — "I thought I would sail about a little" — "I stuffed a shirt or two into my carpet bag, tucked it under my arm, and started for Cape Horn and the Pacific." So it runs, throughout the opening scenes in New Bedford and Nantucket; the characters are real persons, seen through Ishmael's eyes; they speak real speech; the scenes are delineated with subjective realism. Melville is telling a story. His (or Ishmael's) meeting with Queequeg, and their first

night together in the big feather bed at the Spouter Inn, are intensely human and alive. Even Bildad and Peleg are creations of
realism. The first note of fancifulness is introduced with the Ancient
Mariner who accosts Ishmael and Queequeg on the pier in Nantucket. The book, however, still holds to the technical channel of
first person narration; and it is through Ishmael's eyes that one
sees the "Pequod" sail from Nantucket.

Then, without warning, the narrative in Chapter twenty-nine
jumps from the first to the third person; begins to relate conver-
sations which could not possibly have been overheard by Ishmael
and to describe scenes which his eye could not possibly have seen;
follows Ahab into his cabin and Starbuck into the recesses of his
mind, and launches boldly on that sea of mystical soliloquy and
fanciful unreality across which it sweeps for the remainder of the
tale. As it progresses, Ishmael sinks farther and farther from sight,
and the all-seeing eye of the third person comes more and more
into play.

Yet, even at this stage, the technical form of first-person narration is not entirely abandoned; is kept along, as it were, like an
attenuated wraith. As the "Pequod" sights ship after ship, the
narrative momentarily reappears, only to be discarded once more at
the first opportunity; so that, of the main body of the book, it may
truly be said that it is written in both the first and the third persons. For instance, chapter ninety-one, "The 'Pequod' Meets the
'Rosebud' ": "It was a week or two after the last whaling-scene
recounted, and when we [not they] were slowly sailing over a
sleepy, vapoury, midday sea. . . ." This is a recurrence to first person narration in the midst of pages of third-person soliloquy. But
turning to Chapter CXXVIII, "The 'Pequod' Meets the 'Rachel' ":
"Next day, a large ship, the 'Rachel,' was descried, bearing directly
down upon the 'Pequod," all her spars thickly clustering with men"
—this might be either first or third person; the context shows it to
be the latter. Ishmael has been definitely forsaken, and hereafter
remains in abeyance until the end of the book; when, suddenly, he
re-emerges in the epilogue.

The quarrel between the persons, however, does not by any
means comprise the whole technical irregularity of "Moby Dick."
There is the introduction of the form of dramatic dialogue; an inno-
vation singularly successful, and remarkably in keeping both with
the mood of the moment when it is introduced and with the general
tone of mystical formlessness pervading the whole work. There is
the adroit suspending of the narrative by those absorbing chapters

of plain exposition, descriptive of whales and whaling; the gradual revealing of the secrets of the whale, while the final nameless secret is withheld, while fancy and terror feed and grow on suspense. There is the totally ideal development of the characterization, as Ahab and Starbuck and Stubbs and all the rest indulge themselves in the most high-flown and recondite reflections and soliloquies. Finally, there is the bizarre method of chaptering — each chapter a little sketch, each incident having its own chapter; some of the chapters only half a page in length, others a page or two; a hundred and thirty-five chapters in all, together with forewords on etymology and extracts, and an epilogue. In short, "Moby Dick" as a technical exercise is utterly fantastic and original. Melville has departed from every known form of composition; or rather, he has jumbled many forms into a new relation, choosing among them as fancy dictated.

It is safe to say that no literary craftsman of the present day would so much as dream of attempting the experiment which "Moby Dick" discloses on its technical side. Such an attempt would be answered by both critics and public with the ostracism which modern Western culture reserves for irregularity. Here we have a striking commentary on the rigidity of our present literary technique; a technique which rules style and matter, and dominates the literary field, as never before. We speak of ourselves as individualists, freely developing new forms; we like to regard the period of 1840 as a time of stilted and circumscribed literary expression. Yet the truth of the matter seems to be quite otherwise. We are slaves to the success of a literary convention, while the writers of 1840 were relatively free. I am not aware that "Moby Dick" was received at the time of its publication with any degree of surprise at its technical form, whatever surprise or opposition may have been called forth by its content. Neither am I aware that Melville himself felt that he was doing an extraordinary thing in adopting a unique but natural technical form for the expression of an original creative effort. His letters to Hawthorne during the composition of "Moby Dick" betray no self-consciousness on this score. In fact, he seems to have retained a perfectly free relation with his technical medium.

IV

The exhaustion in the latter part of "Moby Dick," of which I have already spoken, seems to me to become startlingly apparent at the crisis of the book, which is reached in the last chapter. Cavilous as the criticism may sound from the viewpoint of a broader appreciation, I sincerely feel that Melville failed to reap in his crisis all that he had sown throughout the body of the tale. The chase of the white whale is splendid; in the daily fight between Ahab and this sinister embodiment of evil Melville is at his best, everything goes magnificently up to the very last; but the final attack of Moby Dick on the ship, and the sinking of the "Pequod" with all her company, are inadequate to the point of anticlimax.

There should have been a more generous descriptive effort at this pass; Melville could picture a scene superbly, and he should have spared no pains to do it here. He seems instead to have adopted an affectation of simplicity. He will rest on his oars now, let the momentum of the book carry it forward, allow the various lines of suspense and horror to culminate of their own accord; in fine, he will sketch the winding up of the piece, leaving the actual descriptive effort to the reader's imagination.

But in this he made a critical error; while it is a fine thing to utilize the reader's imagination, it is disastrous to tax it too far. The last pages of "Moby Dick" do not give us the ending for which we have been prepared; which, with the keenest anticipation, we have been awaiting. Having created such intense suspense, Melville was under the imperative obligation to provide for its satisfaction a flash of equally intense realism. The imagination, having too readily devoured the feast that he has set forth, and finding its hunger only increased thereby, is suddenly let down and disappointed. In this unhappy, defrauded state, it fastens upon the first thing at hand, which is the catastrophe itself; recognizing at once the fantastic nature of that complete oblivion which so causelessly descends on the "Pequod" and her company. For, as a matter of sober fact, a ship of her size would not, in sinking, have drawn down into her vortex an agile cat, much less a crew of whalers, used to being pitched out of boats in the open sea, and surrounded with quantities of dunnage for them to ride when the decks had gone from under.

Turning to the last chapter of "Moby Dick," one may note that it contains but a brief paragraph describing the whale's frantic attack on the vessel. No horror is created, no suspense, no feverish excitement. It is another of art's vanished opportunities. There should have been a close-packed page or two of tumultuous visualization; then, with the gigantic whale dashing head-on toward the devoted "Pequod," a pause in the narrative, to let suspense rankle, while a few paragraphs were occupied with a dissertation on the sinking of vessels — not the sinking of vessels by whales, which matter has already been examined, but the sinking of vessels; about how difficult, how unusual, it would be for a ship to carry her whole company beneath the waves; about Starbuck's knowledge of this fact; about their frantic preparations for escape — then, loosing every ounce of reserve literary power, a description of the crash, the catastrophe, the peculiar and malignant combination of circumstances, easily to be imagined, which, in spite of common experience, did actually destroy this whole ship's company. The whale should have dashed among the debris and floating men, after the ship had gone down, to complete the work of destruction. The scene should have been cast in the form of first-person narration, and Ishmael should have been near enough to see it all. (He was adrift, it will be remembered, and did not go down with the vessel; but the return to the first person is reserved for the epilogue, while the crisis of the story is told in an especially vague form of the third person.) We should have been given a final view of the white whale, triumphantly leaving the scene and resuming the interrupted course of his destiny. In short, there are dozens of strokes of realism neglected in this chapter which plainly demand to be driven home.

Melville chose to end the book on a note of transcendentalism; he himself does not seem to have visualized the scene at all. The influence of Hawthorne, one suspects, was largely responsible for this grave error. Hawthorne was living just over the hill in the Berkshires that summer. The intense and lonely Melville had fallen under his fascination; he thought that he had at last found a friend. He was captivated, also, by that vague imaginative method of thought and style out of which Hawthorne wove his tales; and, quite naturally, his own work reflected this influence. For Melville was that man of genius known as the passionate hunter; he was the taster of all sensations, the searcher of all experience, the sampler of every form and style. And, as so often happens with such people, it was his tragic fate never entirely to find himself. The secret quarry of life constantly eluded him.

The influence of Hawthorne is painfully evident throughout the last two-thirds of "Moby Dick"; painfully evident, because it is so incongruous with Melville's natural manner which is that of narrative realism; he must be there in person — he makes the scene alive with amazing vitality where he stands. In the same sense, his natural power of characterization is in the descriptive or analytical field; I am not aware that he has ever put into the mouth of a single character a realistic speech. Wherever, in "Moby Dick," he gets his best effects, he gets them through the exercise of his natural manner. Certain scenes stand out vividly. Certain pages of analytical characterization are instinct with truth and greatness. The natural impulse keeps bursting through. But the bulk of the characterization is cast in a method artificial to him; he constantly tries to raise the pitch of the tale, to inflate the value of the words. Too much of the descriptive matter likewise is forced through unnatural channels, losing the air of mastery in its adaptation to the less vigorous form of the third person.

Thus the book, in its composition, represents a struggle between realism and mysticism, between a natural and an artificial manner. It begins naturally, it ends artificially. This in a measure explains the strange confusion of the technique, the extravagant use of the two separate persons. Only the most extraordinary creative power could have struck art and achievement from such an alien blend.

What, then, of the allegory?—for we are told that "Moby Dick" is a masterpiece of this form of composition. I must confess that I did not follow the allegory closely, and did not find that it was forced on my attention; and now that I look back on the book, I fail exactly to see wherein it lies. What, for instance, does Ahab represent, and what the white whale? I am not certain that Melville meant the story to be an allegory. In fact, does he not somewhere fiercely disclaim the imputation? But it is the fate of all work done in the manner of transcendentalism to land sooner or later in the rarified atmosphere of allegory, whether it means anything or not, whether or not the allegory seems to point anywhere in particular. Transcendentalism is the stuff of allegory. Melville hated allegory, and would have hated transcendentalism, had he not just then happened to come under the influence of a transcendentalist. This put him in a bad fix, and made him, whether he willed it or not, write a book which looked like allegory. Do we need a better explanation of his turning so fiercely against the imputation?

Not because of its allegorical significance, and not, indeed, because of its mysticism, considered as a thing apart, does this book of the chase of the white whale live among the immortal works of literature; but rather because of its irrepressible triumph of realism over mysticism, because of the inspired and gripping story that builds itself up out of a passionate flow of words. For my part, I like Ahab as Ahab, not as a symbol of something or other; and Ahab lives as Ahab, marvelously enough, in spite of the wild unreality of his constant meditations and ebullitions. Yes, and because of it; the overshadowing demoniac terror of the story lends reality to unreality, charm and substance to mystical formlessness. This is the mark of genius in the creator. Yet even genius may carry things too far; Ahab manages to live as Ahab, but Starbuck—well, Starbuck struts and swells a little, betrayed by an overdose of transcendentalism.

V

If I have seemed to wish that "Moby Dick" had been written in the form of unalloyed narrative realism, that Melville had left off altogether his dalliance with transcendentalism, I would correct the impression now. As a piece of pure realism, the book obviously would not have been the inspired achievement that it is in its present form. The creative struggle that Melville was undergoing at the time of its composition was the intensifying medium through which the work rose to superlative heights. The chapters flow easily, as though he did not realize their duality of form and temper, but felt them to be parts of a unified, continuous product; but the grievous battle taking place within him caused him to produce what actually are gigantic fragments, struck from mountains of fire and anguish, which slowly and ponderously arrange themselves into the delineation of a majestic idea.

"Moby Dick" is not the allegory of Ahab's struggle with destiny; it is rather the story of Melville's struggle with art and life. Without this struggle, there would have been no agonizing greatness; only another "Typee," a splendid tale, a perfect example of literary realism. But, given the struggle, there had to be from page to page this singular conflict in style and form and matter, the confused, reflected gleams of a hidden conflagration; so that to wish the conflict away would be to wish away the book's divinity.

D. H. Lawrence

Herman Melville's "Moby Dick"

Moby Dick, *or the White Whale.*
　A hunt. The last great hunt.
　For what?
　For Moby Dick, the huge white sperm whale: who is old, hoary, monstrous, and swims alone; who is unspeakably terrible in his wrath, having so often been attacked; and snow-white.
　Of course he is a symbol.
　Of what?
　I doubt if even Melville knew exactly. That's the best of it.
　He is warm-blooded, he is loveable. He is lonely Leviathan, not a Hobbes sort. Or is he?
　But he is warm-blooded and loveable. The South Sea Islanders, and Polynesians, and Malays, who worship shark, or crocodile, or weave endless frigate-bird distortions, why did they never worship the whale? So big!
　Because the whale is not wicked. He doesn't bite. And their gods had to bite.

From *Studies in Classic American Literature* by D. H. Lawrence, pp. 145-161. Copyright 1923, renewed 1951 by Frieda Lawrence. Reprinted by permission of The Viking Press, Inc.

He's not a dragon. He is Leviathan. He never coils like the Chinese dragon of the sun. He's not a serpent of the waters. He is warm-blooded, a mammal. And hunted, hunted down.

It is a great book.

At first you are put off by the style. It reads like journalism. It seems spurious. You feel Melville is trying to put something over you. It won't do.

And Melville really is a bit sententious: aware of himself, self-conscious, putting something over even himself. But then it's not easy to get into the swing of a piece of deep mysticism when you just set out with a story.

Nobody can be more clownish, more clumsy and sententiously in bad taste, than Herman Melville, even in a great book like *Moby Dick*. He preaches and holds forth because he's not sure of himself. And he holds forth, often, so amateurishly.

The artist was so *much* greater than the man. The man is rather a tiresome New Englander of the ethical mystical-transcendentalist sort: Emerson, Longfellow, Hawthorne, etc. So unrelieved, the solemn ass even in humour. So hopelessly *au grand sérieux*, you feel like saying: Good God, what does it matter? If life is a tragedy, or a farce, or a disaster, or anything else, what do I care! Let life be what it likes. Give me a drink, that's what I want just now.

For my part, life is so many things I don't care what it is. It's not my affair to sum it up. Just now it's a cup of tea. This morning it was wormwood and gall. Hand me the sugar.

One wearies of the *grand sérieux*. There's something false about it. And that's Melville. Oh dear, when the solemn ass brays! brays! brays!

But he was a deep, great artist, even if he was rather a sententious man. He was a real American in that he always felt his audience in front of him. But when he ceases to be American, when he forgets all audience, and gives us his sheer apprehension of the world, then he is wonderful, his book commands a stillness in the soul, an awe.

In his "human" self, Melville is almost dead. That is, he hardly reacts to human contacts any more; or only ideally: or just for a moment. His human-emotional self is almost played out. He is abstract, self-analytical and abstracted. And he is more spell-bound by the strange slidings and collidings of Matter than by the things men do. In this he is like Dana. It is the material elements he really has to do with. His drama is with them. He was a futurist long before futurism found paint. The sheer naked slidings of the ele-

ments. And the human soul experiencing it all. So often, it is almost
over the border: psychiatry. Almost spurious. Yet so great.

It is the same old thing as in all Americans. They keep their
old-fashioned ideal frock-coat on, and an old-fashioned silk hat,
while they do the most impossible things. There you are: you see
Melville hugged in bed by a huge tattooed South Sea Islander, and
solemnly offering burnt offering to this savage's little idol, and his
ideal frock-coat just hides his shirt-tails and prevents us from
seeing his bare posterior as he salaams, while his ethical silk hat
sits correctly over his brow the while. That is so typically American:
doing the most impossible things without taking off their spiritual
get-up. Their ideals are like armour which has rusted in, and will
never more come off. And meanwhile in Melville his bodily knowledge moves naked, a living quick among the stark elements. For
with sheer physical vibrational sensitiveness, like a marvellous
wireless-station, he registers the effects of the outer world. And he
records also, almost beyond pain or pleasure, the extreme transitions of the isolated, far-driven soul, the soul which is now alone,
without any real human contact. . . .

You would think this relation with Queequeg meant something
to Ishmael. But no. Queequeg is forgotten like yesterday's newspaper. Human things are only momentary excitements or amuse-
ments to the American Ishmael. Ishmael, the hunted. But much
more Ishmael the hunter. What's a Queequeg? What's a wife?
The white whale must be hunted down. Queequeg must be just
"KNOWN", then dropped into oblivion.

And what in the name of fortune is the white whale?

Elsewhere Ishmael says he loved Queequeg's eyes: "large, deep
eyes, fiery black and bold." No doubt like Poe, he wanted to get
the "clue" to them. That was all.

The two men go over from New Bedford to Nantucket, and there
sign on to the Quaker whaling ship, the *Pequod*. It is all strangely
fantastic, phantasmagoric. The voyage of the soul. Yet curiously
a real whaling voyage, too. We pass on into the midst of the sea
with this strange ship and its incredible crew. The Argonauts were
mild lambs in comparison. And Ulysses went *defeating* the Circes
and overcoming the wicked hussies of the isles. But the *Pequod's*
crew is a collection of maniacs fanatically hunting down a lonely,
harmless white whale.

As a soul history, it makes one angry. As a sea yarn, it is marvellous: there is always something a bit over the mark, in sea yarns.
Should be. Then again the masking up of actual seaman's experience

with sonorous mysticism sometimes gets on one's nerves. And again, as a revelation of destiny the book is too deep even for sorrow. Profound beyond feeling.

You are some time before you are allowed to see the captain, Ahab: the mysterious Quaker. Oh, it is a God-fearing Quaker ship.

Ahab, the captain. The captain of the soul.

> "I am the master of my fate,
> I am the captain of my soul!"

Ahab!

"Oh, captain, my captain, our fearful trip is done."

The gaunt Ahab, Quaker, mysterious person, only shows himself after some days at sea. There's a secret about him! What?

Oh, he's a portentous person. He stumps about on an ivory stump, made from sea-ivory. Moby Dick, the great white whale, tore off Ahab's leg at the knee, when Ahab was attacking him.

Quite right, too. Should have torn off both his legs, and a bit more besides.

But Ahab doesn't think so. Ahab is now a monomaniac. Moby Dick is his monomania. Moby Dick must DIE, or Ahab can't live any longer. Ahab is atheist by this.

All right.

This *Pequod*, ship of the American soul, has three mates.

1. Starbuck: Quaker, Nantucketer, a good responsible man of reason, forethought, intrepidity, what is called a dependable man. At the bottom, *afraid*.

2. Stubb: "Fearless as fire, and as mechanical." Insists on being reckless and jolly on every occasion. Must be afraid too, really.

3. Flask: Stubborn, obstinate, without imagination. To him "the wondrous whale was but a species of magnified mouse or water-rat—"

There you have them: a maniac captain and his three mates, three splendid seamen, admirable whalemen, first-class men at their job.

America!

It is rather like Mr. Wilson and his admirable, "efficient" crew, at the Peace Conference. Except that none of the Pequodders took their wives along.

A maniac captain of the soul, and three eminently practical mates.

America!

Then such a crew. Renegades, castaways, cannibals: Ishmael, Quakers.

America!

Three giant harpooners, to spear the great white whale.

1. Queequeg, the South Sea Islander, all tattooed, big and powerful.

2. Tashtego, the Red Indian of the sea-coast, where the Indian meets the sea.

3. Daggoo, the huge black negro.

There you have them, three savage races, under the American flag, the maniac captain, with their great keen harpoons, ready to spear the white whale.

And only after many days at sea does Ahab's own boat-crew appear on deck. Strange, silent, secret, black-garbed Malays, fire-worshipping Parsees. These are to man Ahab's boat, when it leaps in pursuit of that whale.

What do you think of the ship *Pequod,* the ship of the soul of an American?

Many races, many peoples, many nations, under the Stars and Stripes. Beaten with many stripes.

Seeing stars sometimes.

And in a mad ship, under a mad captain, in a mad, fanatic's hunt. For what?

For Moby Dick, the great white whale.

But splendidly handled. Three splendid mates. The whole thing practical, eminently practical in its working. American industry!

And all this practicality in the service of a mad, mad chase.

Melville manages to keep it a real whaling ship, on a real cruise, in spite of all fantastics. A wonderful, wonderful voyage. And a beauty that is so surpassing only because of the author's awful flounderings in mystical waters. He wanted to get metaphysically deep. And he got deeper than metaphysics. It is a surpassingly beautiful book, with an awful meaning, and bad jolts.

It is interesting to compare Melville with Dana, about the albatross — Melville a bit sententious. "I remember the first alba- tross I ever saw. It was during a prolonged gale in waters hard upon the Antarctic seas. From my forenoon watch below I ascended to the overcrowded deck, and there, lashed upon the main hatches, I saw a regal feathered thing of unspotted whiteness, and with a hooked Roman bill sublime. At intervals it arched forth its vast, archangel wings — wondrous throbbings and flutterings shook it. Though bodily unharmed, it uttered cries, as some King's ghost in supernatural distress. Through its inexpressible strange eyes methought I peeped to secrets not below the heavens — the white thing was so white, its wings so wide, and in those for ever exiled waters, I had lost the miserable warping memories of traditions and of towns. I assert then, that in the wondrous bodily whiteness of the bird chiefly lurks the secret of the spell —"

Melville's albatross is a prisoner, caught by a bait on a hook.

Well, I have seen an albatross, too: following us in waters hard upon the Antarctic, too, south of Australia. And in the Southern winter. And the ship, a P. and O. boat, nearly empty. And the lascar crew shivering.

The bird with its long, long wings following, then leaving us. No one knows till they have tried, how lost, how lonely those Southern waters are. And glimpses of the Australian coast.

It makes one feel that our day is only a day. That in the dark of the night ahead other days stir fecund, when we have lapsed from existence.

Who knows how utterly we shall lapse.

But Melville keeps up his disquisition about "whiteness". The great abstract fascinated him. The abstract where we end, and cease to be. White or black. Our white, abstract end! . . .

But it is a great book, a very great book, the greatest book of the sea ever written. It moves awe in the soul.

The terrible fatality.

Fatality.

Doom.

Doom! Doom! Doom! Something seems to whisper it in the very dark trees of America. Doom!

Doom of what?

Doom of our white day. We are doomed, doomed. And the doom is in America. The doom of our white day.

Ah, well, if my day is doomed, and I am doomed with my day, it is something greater than I which dooms me, so I accept my doom as a sign of the greatness which is more than I am.

Melville knew. He knew his race was doomed. His white soul, doomed. His great white epoch, doomed. Himself, doomed. The idealist, doomed. The spirit, doomed.

The reversion. "Not so much bound to any haven ahead, as rushing from all havens astern."

That great horror of ours! It is our civilization rushing from all havens astern.

The last ghastly hunt. The White Whale.

What then is Moby Dick? He is the deepest blood-being of the white race; he is our deepest blood-nature.

And he is hunted, hunted, hunted by the maniacal fanaticism of our white mental consciousness. We want to hunt him down. To subject him to our will. And in this maniacal conscious hunt of ourselves we get dark races and pale to help us, red, yellow, and black, east and west, Quaker and fire-worshipper, we get them all to help us in this ghastly maniacal hunt which is our doom and our suicide.

The last phallic being of the white man. Hunted into the death of upper consciousness and the ideal will. Our blood-self subjected to our will. Our blood-consciousness sapped by a parasitic mental or ideal consciousness.

Hot-blooded sea-born Moby Dick. Hunted by monomaniacs of the idea.

Oh God, oh God, what next, when the *Pequod* has sunk?

She sank in the war, and we are all flotsam.

Now what next?

Who knows? *Quien sabe? Quien sabe, señor?*

Neither Spanish nor Saxon America has any answer.

The *Pequod* went down. And the *Pequod* was the ship of the white American soul. She sank, taking with her negro and Indian and Polynesian, Asiatic and Quaker and good, businesslike Yankees and Ishmael: she sank all the lot of them.

Boom! as Vachel Lindsay would say.

To use the words of Jesus, IT IS FINISHED.

Consummatum est!

But *Moby Dick* was first published in 1851. If the Great White Whale sank the ship of the Great White Soul in 1851, what's been happening ever since?

Post-mortem effects, presumably.

Because, in the first centuries, Jesus was Cetus, the Whale. And the Christians were the litle fishes. Jesus, the Redeemer, was Cetus, Leviathan. And all the Christians all his little fishes.

3. The Try-Works

Henry A. Murray

In Nomine Diaboli

Next to the seizures and shapings of creative thought — the thing itself — no comparable experience is more thrilling than being witched, illumined, and transfigured by the magic of another's art. This is a trance from which one returns refreshed and quickened, and bubbling with unenvious praise of the exciting cause, much as Melville bubbled after his first reading of Hawthorne's *Mosses.* In describing *his* experience Melville chose a phrase so apt — "the shock of recognition" — that in the thirties Edmund Wilson took it as the irresistibly perfect title for his anthology of literary apprecia-tions. Acknowledging a shock of recognition and paying homage to the delivering genius is singularly exhilarating, even today — or especially today — when every waxing enthusiasm must confront an outgoing tide of culture.

In our time, the capacities for wonder and reverence, for generous judgments and trustful affirmations, have largely given way, though not without cause surely, to their antipathies, the humors of a waning ethos: disillusionment, cynicism, disgust, and gnawing envy. These states have bred in us the inclination to dissect the subtlest

From *New England Quarterly*, XXIV (December, 1951), 435-452.

orders of man's wit with ever-sharper instruments of depreciation, to pour all values, the best confounded by the worst, into one mocking-pot, to sneer "realistically," and, as we say today, "assassinate" character. These same humors have disposed writers to spend immortal talent in snickering exhibitions of vulgarity and spiritual emptiness, or in making delicate picture-puzzles out of the butt-ends of life.

In the face of these current trends and tempers, I, coming out of years of brimming gratefulness for the gift of *Moby-Dick*, would like to praise Herman Melville worthily, not to bury him in a winding-sheet of scientific terminology. But the odds are not favorable to my ambition. A commitment of thirty years to analytic modes of thought and concepts lethal to emotion has built such habits in me that were I to be waked in the night by a cry of "Help!" I fear I would respond in the lingo of psychology. I am suffering from one of the commonest ailments of our age—trained disability.

The habit of a psychologist is to break down the structure of each personality he studies into elements, and so in a few strokes to bring to earth whatever merit that structure, as a structure, may possess. Furthermore, for reasons I need not mention here, the technical terms for the majority of these elements have derogatory connotations. Consequently, it is difficult to open one's professional mouth without disparaging a fellow-being. Were an analyst to be confronted by that much-heralded but still missing specimen of the human race—the normal man—he would be struck dumb, for once, through lack of appropriate ideas.

If I am able to surmount to some extent any impediments of this origin, you may attribute my good fortune to a providential circumstance. In the procession of my experiences *Moby-Dick* anteceded Psychology, that is, I was swept by Melville's gale and shaken by his appalling sea dragon before I had acquired the all-leveling academic oil that is poured on brewed-up waters, and before I possessed the weapons and tools of science—the conceptual lance, harpoons, cutting iron, and what-nots—which might have reduced the "grand hooded phantom" to mere blubber. Lacking these defenses I was whelmed. Instead of my changing this book, this book changed me.

To me, *Moby-Dick* was Beethoven's *Eroica* in words: first of all, a masterly orchestration of harmonic and melodic language, of resonating images and thoughts in varied metres. Equally compelling were the spacious sea-setting of the story, the cast of characters and their prodigious common target, the sorrow, the fury, and the terror, together with all those frequent touches, those subtle interminglings of unexampled humor, quizzical and, in the American way, extravagant, and finally the fated closure, the crown and tragic consummation of the immense yet firmly-welded whole. But still more extraordinary and portentous were the penetration and scope, the sheer audacity of the author's imagination. Here was a man who did not fly away with his surprising fantasies to some unbelievable dreamland, pale or florid, shunning the stubborn objects and gritty facts, the prosaic routines and practicalities of everyday existence. Here was a man who, on the contrary, chose these very things as vessels for his procreative powers — the whale as a naturalist, a Hunter or a Cuvier, would perceive him, the business of killing whales, the whale-ship running as an oil factory, stowing-down, in fact, every mechanism and technique, each tool and gadget, that was integral to the money-minded industry of whaling. Here was a man who could describe the appearance, the concrete matter-of-factness, and the utility of each one of these natural objects, implements, and tools with the fidelity of a scientist, and, while doing this, explore it as a conceivable respository of some aspect of the human drama; then, by an imaginative tour de force, deliver a vital essence, some humorous or profound idea, coalescing with its embodiment. But still more. Differing from the symbolists of our time, here was a man who offered us essences and meanings which did not level or depreciate the objects of his contemplation. On the contrary, this loving man exalted all creatures — the mariners, renègades, and castaways on board the *Pequod* — by ascribing to them "high qualities, though dark" and weaving round them "tragic graces." Here, in short, was a man with the myth-making powers of a Blake, a hive of significant associations, who was capable of reuniting what science had put asunder — pure perception and relevant emotion — and doing it in an exultant way that was acceptable to skepticism.

Not at first, but later, I perceived the crucial difference between Melville's dramatic animations of nature and those of primitive religion-makers: both were spontaneous and uncalculated projections, but Melville's were in harmony, for the most part, with scientific knowledge, because they had been recognized as projections, checked, and modified. Here, then, was a man who might redeem us from the virtue of an incredible subjective belief, on the one side, and from the virtue of a deadly objective rationality, on the other.

For these and other reasons the reading of *Moby-Dick*—coming before Psychology—left a stupendous reverberating imprint, too lively to be diminished by the long series of relentless analytical operations to which I subsequently subjected it. Today, after twenty-five years of such experiments, *The Whale* is still *the* whale, more magnificent, if anything, than before.

Before coming to grips with the "mystery" of *Moby-Dick* I should mention another providential circumstance to which all psychologists are, or should be, forever grateful, and literary critics too, since without it no complete understanding of books like *Moby-Dick* would be possible today. Ahead of us were two greatly gifted pioneers, Freud and Jung, who with others, explored the manifold vagaries of unconscious mental processes and left for our inheritance their finely-written works. The discoveries of these adventurers advantaged me in a special way: they gave, I thought, support to one of Santayana's early convictions, that in the human being imagination is more fundamental than perception. Anyhow, adopting this position, some of us psychologists have been devoting ourselves to the study of dreams, fantasies, creative productions, and projections—all of which are primarily and essentially emotional and dramatic, such stuff as myths are made of. Thus, by chance or otherwise, this branch of the tree of psychology is growing in the direction of Herman Melville.

To be explicit: psychologists have been recognizing in the dream figures and fantasy figures of today's children and adolescents more and more family likenesses of the heroes and heroines of primitive myths, legends, and fables—figures, in other words, who are engaged in comparable heroic strivings and conflicts, and experiencing comparable heroic triumphs or fatalities. Our ancestors, yielding to an inherent propensity of the mind, projected the more relevant of these figures into objects of their environment, into sun, moon, and stars, into the unknown deeps of the sea and of the earth, and into the boundless void of heaven; and they worshipped the most potent of these projected images, whether animal or human, as super-beings, gods, or goddesses. On any clear night one can see scores of the more luminous of such divinities parading up and down the firmament. For example, in Fall and Winter, one looks with admiration on that resplendent hero Perseus and above him the chained beauty, Andromeda, whom he saved from a devouring monster, ferocious as Moby Dick. Now, what psychologists have been learning by degrees is that Perseus is in the unconscious mind of every man and Andromeda in every woman, not, let me hasten

to say, as an inherited fixed image, but as a potential set of dispositions which may be constellated in the personality by the occurrence
of a certain kind of situation. Herman Melville arrived at this
conclusion in his own way a hundred years ago, sooner and, I
believe, with more genuine comprehension than any other writer.

An explanation of all this in scientific terms would require all the
space permitted me and more. Suffice it to say here that the
psychologists who are studying the elementary myth-makings of
the mind are dealing with the germy sources of poetry and drama,
the fecundities out of which great literature is fashioned. Futher-
more, in attempting to formulate and classify these multifarious
productions of the imagination, the psychologist uses modes of
analysis and synthesis very similar to those that Aristotle used in
setting forth the dynamics of Greek tragedy. In these and other
trends I find much encouragement for the view that a rapproche-
ment of psychology and literary criticism is in progress, and that
it will prove fruitful to both callings. As an ideal meeting ground I
would propose Melville's world of "wondrous depths."

To this Columbus of the mind, the great archetypal figures of
myth, drama, and epic were not pieces of intellectual Dresden china,
heirlooms of a classical education, ornamental bric-a-brac to be put
here and there for the pleasure of genteel readers. Many of the
more significant of these constellations were inwardly experienced
by Melville, one after the other, as each was given vent to blossom
and assert itself. Thus, we are offered a spectacle of spiritual development through passionate identifications. Only by proceeding in
this way could Melville have learnt on his pulses what it was to
be Narcissus, Orestes, Oedipus, Ishmael, Apollo, Lucifer. "Like a
frigate," he said, "I am full with a thousand souls."

This brings me to the problem of interpreting *Moby-Dick*. Some
writers have said that there is nothing to interpret: it is a plain sea
story marred here and there by irrelevant ruminations. But I shall
not cite the abundant proof for the now generally accepted proposition that in *Moby-Dick* Melville "meant" something — something,
I should add, which he considered "terrifically true" but which, in
the world's judgment, was so harmful "that it were all but madness
for any good man, in his own proper character, to utter or even
hint of." What seems decisive here is the passage in Melville's
celebrated letter to Hawthorne: "A sense of unspeakable security
is in me this moment, on account of your having understood the
book." From this we can conclude that there *are* meanings to be
understood in *Moby-Dick*, and also — may we say for our own

encouragement?—that Melville's ghost will feel secure forever if modern critics can find them, and, since Hawthorne remained silent, set them forth in print. Here it might be well to remind ourselves of a crucial statement which follows the just quoted passage from Melville's letter: "I have written a wicked book." The implication is clear: all interpretations which fail to show that *Moby-Dick* is, in some sense, wicked have missed the author's avowed intention.

A few critics have scouted all attempts to fish Melville's own meaning out of *The Whale*, on the ground that an interpretation of a work of art so vast and so complex is bound to be composed in large measure of projections from the mind of the interpreter. It must be granted that preposterous projections often do occur in the course of such an effort. But these are not inevitable. Self-knowledge and discipline may reduce projections to a minimum. Anyhow, in the case of *Moby-Dick*, the facts do not sustain the proposition that a critic can see nothing in this book but his own reflected image. The interpretations which have been published over the last thirty years exhibit an unmistakable trend towards consensus in respect to the drama as a whole as well as many of its subordinate parts. Moreover, so far as I can judge, the critics who, with hints from their predecessors, applied their intuitions most recently to the exegesis of *The Whale*, can be said to have arrived, if taken together, at Melville's essential meaning. Since one or another of these authors has deftly said what I clumsily thought, my prejudices are strongly in favor of their conclusions, and I am whole-hearted in applauding them, Mr. Arvin's[1] most especially, despite their having left me with nothing fresh to say. Since this is how things stand, my version of the main theme of *Moby-Dick* can be presented in a briefer form, and limited to two hypotheses.

The first of them is this: Captain Ahab is an embodiment of that fallen angel or demi-god who in Christendom was variously named Lucifer, Devil, Adversary, Satan. The Church Fathers would have called Captain Ahab "Antichrist" because he was not Satan himself, but a human creature possessed of all Satan's pride and energy, "summing up within himself," as Irenaeus said, "the apostasy of the devil."

That it was Melville's intention to beget Ahab in Satan's image can hardly be doubted. He told Hawthorne that his book had been boiled in hell-fire and secretly baptized not in the name of God but in the name of the Devil. He named his tragic hero after the Old

---

[1]Newton Arvin, *Herman Melville* (New York, 1950).

Testament ruler who "did more to provoke the Lord God of Israel
to anger than all the Kings of Israel that were before him." King
Ahab's accuser, the prophet Elijah, is also resurrected to play his
original rôle, though very briefly, in Melville's testament. We are
told that Captain Ahab is an "ungodly, god-like" man who is
spiritually outside Christendom. He is a well of blasphemy and
defiance, of scorn and mockery for the gods — "cricket-players and
pugilists" in his eyes. Rumor has it that he once spat in the holy
goblet on the altar of the Catholic Church at Santa. "I never saw
him keel," says Stubb. He is associated in the text with scores of
references to the Devil. He is an "anaconda of an old man." His
self-assertive sadism is the linked antithesis of the masochistic
submission preached by Father Mapple.

Captain Ahab-Lucifer is also related to a sun-god, like Christ,
but in reverse. Instead of being light leaping out of darkness, he is
"darkness leaping out of light." The *Pequod* sails on Christmas
Day. *This* new year's sun will be the god of Wrath rather than
the god of Love. Ahab does not emerge from his subterranean
abode until his ship is "rolling through the bright Quito spring"
(Easter-tide, symbolically, when the all-fertilizing sun-god is resurrected). The frenzied ceremony in which Ahab's followers are sworn
to the pursuit of the White Whale — "Commend the murderous
chalices!" — is suggestive of the Black Mass; the lurid operations
at the try-works is a scene out of Hell.

There is some evidence that Melville was re-reading *Paradise
Lost* in the summer of 1850, shortly after, let us guess, he got the
idea of transforming the captain of his whale-ship into the first of
all cardinal sinners who fell by pride. Anyhow, Melville's Satan is
the spitting image of Milton's hero, but portrayed with deeper and
subtler psychological insight, and placed where he belongs, in the
heart of an enraged man.

Melville may have been persuaded by Goethe's Mephistopheles,
or even by some of Hawthorne's bloodless abstracts of humanity,
to add Fedallah to his cast of characters. Evidently he wanted to
make certain that no reader would fail to recognize that Ahab had
been possessed by, or had sold his soul to, the Devil. Personally, I
think Fedallah's rôle is superfluous and I regret that Melville made
room for him and his unbelievable boat-crew on the ship *Pequod*.
Still, he is not wholly without interest. He represents the cool,
heartless, cunning, calculating, intellectual Devil of the Medieval
myth-makers, in contrast, to the stricken, passionate, indignant,

and often eloquent rebel angel of *Paradise Lost,* whose rôle is played by Ahab.

The Arabic name "Fedallah" suggests "dev(il) Allah," that is, the Mohammedans' god as he appeared in the mind's eye of a Crusader. But we are told that Fedallah is a Parsee — a Persian fire-worshipper, or Zoroastrian, who lives in India. Thus, Ahab, named after the Semitic apostate who was converted to the orgiastic cult of Baal, or Bel, originally a Babylonian fertility god, has formed a compact with a Zoroastrian whose name reminds us of still another Oriental religion. In addition, Captain Ahab's whale-boat is manned by a crew of unregenerate infidels, as defined by orthodox Christianity, and each of his three harpooners, Queequeg, Tastego, and Daggoo, is a member of a race which believed in other gods than the one god of the Hebraic-Christian Bible.

Speaking roughly, it might be said that Captain Ahab, incarnation of the Adversary and master of the ship *Pequod* (named after the aggressive Indian tribe that was exterminated by the Puritans of New England), has summoned the various religions of the East to combat the one dominant religion of the West. Or, in other terms, that he and his followers, Starbuck excepted, represent the horde of primitive drives, values, beliefs, and practises which the Hebraic-Christian religionists rejected and excluded, and by threats, punishments, and inquisitions, forced into the unconscious mind of Western man.

Stated in psychological concepts, Ahab is captain of the culturally repressed dispositions of human nature, that part of personality which psychoanalysts have termed the "Id." If this is true, his opponent, the White Whale, can be none other than the internal institution which is responsible for these repressions, namely the Freudian Superego. This then is my second hypothesis: Moby-Dick is a veritable spouting, breaching, sounding whale, a whale who, because of his whiteness, his mighty bulk and beauty, and because of one instinctive act that happened to dismember his assailant, has received the projection of Captain Ahab's Presbyterian conscience, and so may be said to embody the Old Testament Calvinistic conception of an affrighting Deity and his strict commandments, the derivative puritan ethic of nineteenth-century America, and the society that defended this ethic. Also, and most specifically, he symbolizes the zealous parents whose righteous sermonizings and corrections drove the prohibitions in so hard that a serious young man could hardly reach outside the barrier, except possibly far away among some tolerant, gracious Polynesian peoples. The emphasis should be placed on that unconscious (and hence inscrutable) wall of inhibition which imprisoned the puritan's thrusting passions. "How can the prisoner reach outside," cries Ahab, "except by thrusting through the wall? To me, the White Whale is that wall, shoved near to me . . . I see in him outrageous strength, with an inscrutable malice sinewing it." As a symbol of a sounding, breaching, white-dark, unconquerable New England conscience what could be better than a sounding, breaching, white-dark, unconquerable sperm whale?

Who is the psychoanalyst who could resist the immediate inference that the *imago* of the mother as well as the *imago* of the father is contained in the Whale? In the present case there happens to be a host of biographical facts and written passages which support this proposition. Luckily, I need not review them, because Mr. Arvin and others have come to the same conclusion. I shall confine myself to one reference. It exhibits Melville's keen and sympathetic insight into the cultural determinants of his mother's prohibiting dispositions. In *Pierre*, it is the "high-up, and towering and all-forbidding . . . edifice of his mother's immense pride . . . her pride of birth . . . her pride of purity," that is the "wall shoved near," the wall that stands between the hero and the realization of his heart's resolve. But instead of expending the fury of frustration upon his mother, he directs it at Fate, or, more specifically, at his mother's God and the society that shaped her. For he saw "that not his mother had made his mother; but the Infinite Haughtines had first fashioned her; and then the haughty world had further molded her; nor had a haughty Ritual omitted to finish her."

Given this penetrating apprehension we are in a position to say that Melville's target in *Moby-Dick* was the upper middle-class culture of his time. It was *this* culture which was defended with righteous indignation by what he was apt to call "the world" or "the public," and Melville had very litle respect for "the world" or "the public." The "public," or men operating as a social system, was something quite distinct from "the people." In *White Jacket* he wrote: "The public and the people! . . . let us hate the one, and cleave to the other." "The public is a monster," says Lemsford. Still earlier Melville had said: "I fight against the armed and crested lies of Mardi (the world)." "Mardi is a monster whose eyes are fixed in its head, like a whale." Many other writers have used similar imagery. Sir Thomas Browne referred to the multitude as "that numerous piece of monstrosity"; Keats spoke of "the dragon world." But closest of all was Hobbes: "By art is created that great Leviathan, called a commonwealth or state." It was in the laws of this Leviathan, Hobbes made clear, that the sources of right and wrong reside. To summarize: the giant mass of Melville's whale is the same as Melville's man-of-war world, the *Neversink*, in *White Jacket*, which in turn is an epitome of Melville's Mardi. The Whale's white forehead and hump should be reserved for the world's heavenly King.

That God is incarnate in the Whale has been perceived by Mr. Stone,[2] and, as far as I know, by every other Catholic critic of Melville's work, as well as by several Protestant critics. In fact, Mr. Chase[3] has marshalled so fair a portion of the large bulk of evidence on this point that any more from me would be superfluous. Of course, what Ahab projects into the Whale is not the image of a loving Father, but the God of the Old Dispensation, the God who brought Jeremiah into darkness, hedged him about, and made his path crooked; the God, adopted by the fire-and-brimstone Puritans, who said: "With fury poured out I will rule over you." "The sword without and the terror within, shall destroy both the young man and the virgin." "I will also send the teeth of beasts upon them." "I will heap mischiefs upon them." "To me belongeth vengence and recompense."

Since the society's vision of deity, and the society's morality, and the parents and ministers who implant these conceptions, are represented in a fully socialized personality by an establishment that is called the Superego — Conscience as Freud defined it —, and since Ahab has been proclaimed "Captain of the Id," the simplest psychological formula for Melville's dramatic epic is this: an insurgent Id in mortal conflict with an oppressive cultural Superego. Starbuck, the First Mate, stands for the rational realistic Ego which is overpowered by the fanatical compulsiveness of the Id and dispossessed of its normally regulating functions.

If this is approximately correct, it appears that while writing his greatest work Melville abandoned his detached position in the Ego from time to time, hailed "the realm of shades," as his hero Taji had, and, through the mediumship of Ahab, "burst his hot heart's shell" upon the sacrosanct Almighty and the sacrosanct sentiments of Christendom. Since in the world's judgment, 1851, nothing could be more reproachable than this, it would be unjust, if not treacher-

---

[2]Geoffrey Stone, *Melville* (New York, 1949).
[3]Richard Volney Chase, *Herman Melville: A Critical Study* (New York, 1949).

ous, of us to reason *Moby-Dick* into some comforting morality play
for which no boldness was required. This would be depriving Melville of the ground he gained for self-respect by having dared to
abide by his own subjective truth and write a "wicked book," the
kind of book that Pierre's publishers, Steel, Flint, and Asbestos,
would have called "a blasphemous rhaspsody filched from the vile
Atheists, Lucian and Voltaire."

Some may wonder how it was that Melville, a fundamentally
good, affectionate, noble, idealistic, and reverential man, should
have felt impelled to write a wicked book. Why did he aggress so
furiously against Western orthodoxy, as furiously as Byron and
Shelley, or any Satanic writer who preceded him, as furiously as
Nietzsche or the most radical of his sucessors in our day?

In *Civilization and its Discontents* Freud, out of the ripeness of
his full experience, wrote that when one finds deep-seated aggression — and by this he meant aggression of the sort that Melville
voiced — one can safely attribute it to the frustration of Eros. In
my opinion this generalization does not hold for all men of all
cultures at all times, but the probability of its being valid is
extremely high in the case of an earnest, moralistic, nineteenth-
century American, a Presbyterian to boot, whose anger is born of
suffering, especially if this man spent an impressionable year of his
life in Polynesia and returned to marry the very proper little daughter of the Chief Justice of Massachusetts, and if, in addition, he is
a profoundly creative man in whose androgynic personality mascu-
line and feminine components are integrally blended.

If it were concerned with *Moby-Dick*, the book, rather than with
its author, I would call *this* my third hypothesis: Ahab-Melville's
aggression was directed against the object that once harmed Eros
with apparent malice and was still thwarting it with presentiments
of further retaliations. The correctness of this inference is indicated
by the nature of the injury — a symbolic emasculation — that excited Ahab's ire. Initially, this threatening object was, in all likeli-
hood, the father, later, possibly, the mother. But, as Melville plainly
saw, both his parents had been fashioned by the Hebraic-Christian,
American Calvinist tradition, the tradition which conceived of a
deity in whose eyes Eros was depravity. It was the first Biblical
myth-makers who dismissed from heaven and from earth the Great
Goddess of the Oriental and primitive religions, and so rejected
the feminine principle as a spiritual force. Ahab, protagonist of
these rejected religions, in addressing heaven's fire and lightning,

what he calls "the personified impersonal," cries: "But thou art my fiery father; my sweet mother I know not. Oh, cruel! What hast thou done with her?" He calls this god a foundling, a "hermit immemorial," who does not know his own origin. Again, it was the Hebraic authors, sustained later by the Church Fathers, who propagated the legend that a woman was the cause of Adam's exile from Paradise, and that the original sin was concupiscence. Melville says that Ahab, spokesman of all exiled princes, "piled upon the whale's white hump the sum of all the general rage and hate felt by his whole race from Adam down." Remember also that it was the lure of Jezebel that drew King Ahab of Israel outside the orthodoxy of his religion and persuaded him to worship the Phoenician Astarte, goddess of love and fruitful increase. "Jezebel" was the worst tongue-lash a puritan could give a woman. She was Sex, and sex was Sin, spelled with a capital. It was the Church periodicals of Melville's day that denounced *Typee*, called the author a sensualist, and influenced the publishers to delete suggestive passages from the second edition. It was this long heritage of aversion and animosity, so accentuated in this country, which banned sex relations as a topic of discourse and condemned divorce as an unpardonable offense. All this has been changed, for better and for worse, by the moral revolutionaries of our own time who, feeling as Melville felt but finding the currents of sentiment less strongly opposite, spoke out, and with their wit, indignation, and logic, reinforced by the findings of psychoanalysis, disgraced the stern-faced idols of their forebears. One result is this: today an incompatible marriage is not a prison-house, as it was for Melville, "with wall shoved near."

In *Pierre* Melville confessed his own faith when he said that Eros is god of all, and Love "the loftiest religion of this earth." To the romantic Pierre the image of Isabel was "a silent and tyrannical call, challenging him in his deepest moral being, and summoning Truth, Love, Pity, Conscience to the stand." Here he seems to have had in mind the redeeming and inspiring Eros of Courtly Love, a heresy which the Medieval Church had done its utmost to stamp out. *This*, he felt convinced, was *his* "path to God," although in the way of it he saw with horror the implacable conscience and worldly valuations of his revered mother.

If this line of reasoning is as close as I think it is to the known facts, then Melville, in the person of Ahab, assailed Calvinism in the Whale because it blocked the advance of a conscience beneficent to evolutionary love. And so, weighed in the scales of its creator, *Moby-Dick* is not a wicked book but a *good* book, and after finishing it Melville had full reason to feel, as he confessed, "spotless as the lamb."

But then, seen from another point, *Moby-Dick* might be judged a wicked book, not because its hero condemns an entrenched tradition, but because he is completely committed to destruction. Although Captain Ahab manifests the basic stubborn virtues of the arch-protestant and the rugged individualist carried to their limits, *this* god-defier is no Prometheus, since all thought of benefiting humanity is foreign to him. His purpose is not to make the Pacific safe for whaling, nor, when blasting at the moral order, does he have in mind a more heartening vision for the future. The religion of Eros which might once have been the secret determinant of Ahab's undertaking is never mentioned. At one critical point in *Pierre* the hero-author, favored by a flash of light, exclaims, "I will gospelize the world anew"; but he never does. Out of light comes darkness: the temper of Pierre's book is no different from the temper of *Moby-Dick*. The truth is that Ahab is motivated solely by his private need to avenge a private insult. His governing philosophy is that of nihilism, the doctrine that the existing system must be shattered. Nihilism springs up when the imagination fails to provide the redeeming solution of an unbearable dilemma, when "the creative response," as Toynbee would say, is not forthcoming, and a man reacts out of a hot heart—"to the dogs with the head"— and swings to an instinct—"the same that prompts even a worm to turn under the heel." This is what White Jacket did when arraigned at the mast, and what Pierre did when fortune deserted him, and what Billy Budd did when confronted by his accuser. "Nature has not implanted any power in man," said Melville, "that was not meant to be exercised at times, though too often our powers have been abused. The privilege, inborn and inalienable, that every man has, of dying himself and inflicting death upon another, was not given to us without a purpose. These are the last resources of an insulted and unendurable existence."

If we grant that Ahab is a wicked man, what does this prove? It proves that *Moby-Dick* is a *good* book, a parable in epic form, because Melville makes a great spectacle of Ahab's wickedness and shows through the course of the narrative how such wickedness will drive a man on iron rails to an appointed nemesis. Melville adherred to the classic formula for tragedies. He could feel "spotless as the lamb," because he had seen to it that the huge threat to the social system, immanent in Ahab's two cardinal defects—egotistic self-inflation and unleashed wrath — was, at the end, fatefully exterminated, "and the great shroud of the sea rolled on as it rolled five thousand years ago." The reader has had his catharsis, equilibrium has been restored, sanity is vindicated.

This is true, but is it the whole truth? In point of fact, while writing *Moby-Dick* did Melville maintain aesthetic distance, keeping his own feelings in abeyance? Do we not hear Ahab saying things that the later Pierre will say and that Melville said less vehemently in his own person? Does not the author show marked partiality for the "mightly pageant creature" of his invention, put in *his* mouth the finest, boldest language? Also, have not many interpreters been so influenced by the abused Ahab that they saw nothing in his opponent but the source of all malicious agencies, the very Devil? As Mr. Mumford has said so eloquently, Ahab is at heart a noble being whose tragic wrong is that of battling against evil with "power instead of love," and so becoming "the image of the thing he hates." With this impression imbedded in our minds, how can we come out with any moral except this: evil wins. We admit that Ahab's wickedness has been cancelled. But what survives? It is the much more formidable, compacted wickedness of the group that survives, the world that is "saturated and soaking with lies," and their man-of-war God, who is hardly more admirable than a primitive totem beast, some oral-aggressive, child-devouring Cronos of the sea. Is this an idea that a man of good-will can rest with?

Rest with? Certainly not. Meville's clear intention was to bring not rest, but *unrest* to intrepid minds. All gentle people were warned away from his book "on risk of a lumbago or sciatica." "A polar wind blows through it," he announced. He had not written to soothe, but to kindle, to make men leap from their seats, as Whitman would say, and fight for their lives. Was it the poet's function to buttress the battlements of complacency, to give comfort to the enemy? There is little doubt about the nature of the enemy in Melville's day. It was the dominant idealogy, that peculiar compound of puritanism and materialism, of rationalism and commercialism, of shallow, blatant optimism and technology, which proved so crushing to creative evolutions in religion, art, and life. In such circumstances every "true poet," as Blake said, "is of the Devil's party," whether he knows it or not. Surveying the last hundred and fifty years, how many exceptions to this statement can we find? Melville, anyhow, knew that *he* belonged to the party, and while writing *Moby-Dick* so gloried in his membership that he baptized his work *In Nomine Diaboli*. It was precisely under these auspices that he created his solitary masterpiece, a construction of the same high order as the Constitution of the United States and the scientific treatises of Willard Gibbs, though huge and wild and unruly as the Grand Canyon. And it is for this marvel chiefly that he resides in our hearts now among the greatest in "that small but high-hushed world" of bestowing geniuses.

Here ends this report of my soundings in *Moby-Dick*. The drama is finshed. What became of its surviving author?

Moby-Dick may be taken as a comment on the strategic crisis of Melville's allegorical life. In portraying the consequences of Ahab's last suicidal lunge, the hero's umbilical fixation to the Whale and his death by strangling, the author signalized not only his permanent attachment to the *imago* of the mother, but the submission he had foreseen to the binding power of the parental conscience, the Superego of middle-class America. Measured against the standards of *his* day, then, Melville must be accounted a *good* man.

But does this entitle him to a place on the side of the angels? He abdicated to the conscience he condemned and his ship *Pequod*, in sinking, carried down with it the conscience he aspired to, represented by the sky-hawk, the bird of heaven. With his ideal drowned, life from then on was load and time stood still. All he had denied to love he gave throughout a martyrdom of forty years, to death.

But "hark ye yet again — the little lower layer." Melville's capitulation in the face of overwhelming odds was limited to the sphere of action. His embattled soul refused surrender and lived on, breathing back defiance, disputing "to the last gasp" of his "earthquake life" the sovereignty of that inscrutable authority in him. As he wrote in *Pierre*, unless the enthusiast "can find the talismanic secret, to reconcile this world with his own soul, then there is no peace for him, no slighest truce for him in this life." Years later we find him holding the same ground. "Terrible is earth" was his conclusion, but despite all, "no retreat through me." By this dogged stand he bequeathed to succeeding generations the unsolved problem of the talismanic secret.

Only at the very last, instinct spent, earthquake over, did he fall back to a position close to Christian resignation. In his Being, was not this man "a wonder, a grandeur, and a woe?"

Howard C. Horsford

The Design of the
Argument in *Moby-Dick*

The predatory white spider of Frost's sonnet "Design" may seem little akin to a white whale, yet the final question which the poem suggests makes a pointed epigraph for Melville's novel:

> What but design of darkness to appall?—
> If design govern in a thing so small.

Metaphysics spans greater leaps; Frost and Melville are but two of many who have questioned the universal whole in the riddling part. It is the obverse side of a long intellectual tradition in western religious consciousness—a tradition notable in America for its Protestant intensity. This intenser manifestation the foremost scholar of the New England mind has described as "the Puritan's effort to confront, face to face, the image of a blinding divinity in the physical universe," without mediation, without priest or ritual.[1]

The linking of God and nature still exercises a tenacious hold on our thinking. Only a few years ago, Frank Lloyd Wright buoyantly

From *Modern Fiction Studies*, VIII (Autumn, 1962), 233-251. *Modern Fiction Studies*, © 1962 by Purdue Research Foundation, Lafayette, Indiana.
[1]Perry Miller, headnote to the reprinting of "From Edwards to Emerson," in his *Errand into the Wilderness* (Cambridge, Mass., 1956), p. 185.

assured the young ladies graduating from Sarah Lawrence College, "I think Nature should be spelled with a capital 'N', not because Nature is God but because all that we can learn of God we will learn from the body of God, which we call Nature." A respectable scientific symposium offers "The Evidence of God in an Expanding Universe," while a popular dramatist in a popular magazine stands agape at "the Master Mechanic who laid the tracks for our space ships."[2]

But the audience which Melville's novel now finds is not likely to share Mr. Wright's ebullient certainty, or Mr. Hecht's amazement, or even the assurance of "Forty American Scientists" (however reputable in their own fields) that an orderly universe evidences a beneficent, an intelligible deity delighting in His creation. Not in itself, of course, a systematic statement of philosophical and religious arguments, *Moby-Dick* nevertheless is the response of a powerful imagination to the intellectual disintegration of faith.

Let use concede at once that we are not dealing here with a mind disciplined in academic philosophy, though Melville read omnivorously; let us agree that, though it is a great novel, *Moby-Dick* does not conform to the traditional conventions of fiction, or even that it has distressing lapses in craftsmanship. We are not concerned with that here. Yet it is as a profoundly imaginative artist that Melville responds to the impact of new ideas on belief; as an artist he sensed fully — more fully perhaps than any other novelist, certainly in English — the profundity of that impact as vital experience. His rendering of *that* is what a reader must deal with ultimately.

A novel so richly conceived, certainly, demands the awareness of many considerations, but only with this ultimate consideration in mind, I think, can we comprehend the magnitude and the genuine nature of Ahab's tragedy, can we make sense out of the function of Ishmael. It is not new to point to Melville's life-long concern with the relation between knowledge and belief, but we need to explore more fully his imaginative rendering of the implications of such a relationship — and its collapse — if we are to understand better our response to his fiction.

Though religious faith and Biblical literalism had much to suffer from science later in the nineteenth century, Melville grew up with

---

[2] *The New Yorker*, XXXIV (June 14, 1958), 27; John Clover Monsma, ed., *The Evidence of God in an Expanding Universe: Forty American Scientists Declare their Affirmative Views on Religion* (New York, 1958); Ben Hecht, in *Esquire*, L (November, 1958), 68.

the generations still wracked by the new theory of knowledge developed most fully by David Hume. In the face of the pious complacencies of the "Age of Reason," Hume had argued that nothing can be discovered by reasoning on the subjects with which metaphysics is concerned. Mere custom, only, stands warrant for our ideas of cause and effect; "belief" is not "knowledge" and "is more properly an act of the sensitive, than of the cogitative part of our natures."[3]

It may be true, as I have heard it said, that no one in the nineteenth century really understood Hume, the "Scotch Goliath," as Emerson called him; nevertheless, concerning that subject which seems to have touched nineteenth-century man most closely, religious belief, those young men of Emerson's and Melville's generations — those who thought about it at all — sensed profoundly enough the desperate implications of Hume's skeptical epistemology. "Who is he that can stand up before him," the deeply troubled young Emerson asked his aunt, "& prove the existence of the Universe, & of its Founder?"[4]

This is the problem which for Melville so largely shapes the "ontological heroics" (the phrase is his) he passionately argued those years — not the new geology, not the emerging new biology, but the consequences of the new epistemology. For Hume, in arguing the purely subjective, the illusory nature of knowledge, had struck at a rooted habit of thought, one conditioned by milleniums of tradition in the western religious world, one which had almost immemorially asserted the nature and providence of God on the material evidence of His handiwork.

From the Psalmists and St. Paul to Bishops Butler and Paley there was indisputable authority to justify the habit of investing nature with symbolic significance, of finding analogy, evidence, even proof of the Creator in His creation. It is a commonplace of intellectual history to point to the devout Newton's notion of the universe as a vast cryptogram set by the Almighty for man to decipher, or to the many arguments from design flowering complacently in the light of eighteenth-century science. Deist and orthodox alike delighted in the illumination the "light of nature" shed on Divinity, differing chiefly only in the degree of sufficiency accorded such revelation.

---

[3]See, for example, the arguments in Part III, "Of Knowledge and Probability," *A Treatise of Human Nature.*

[4]Letter to Mary Moody Emerson, October 16, 1823, *Letters of Ralph Waldo Emerson,* ed. Ralph L. Rusk, 6 vols. (New York, 1939); I, 138.

If the conservative qualified "natural revelation" by a due suspicion of the post-lapsarian world, others more recently shaken shouted their faith in the stridency of renewed vision, like Carlyle's trumpeted revelation in *Sartor Resartus*, "The Universe is but one vast Symbol of God."[5] But suppose our "knowledge" of this universe, which presumably so manifests its Creator, should be, after all, only subjectively created illusion, delusory? The profound implications in this possibility were what so challenged the imagination of the returned young sailor just discovering the exciting world of the mind. And this is an America where, as so many have shown, the divinely benign influence of nature on the heroic new men of this new Eden was likely to be proclaimed in any editorial, in any patriotic oration, alike from the orthodox pulpit and the lyceum platform of the self-styled transcendentalists.

Thus, though they by no means define between them all the aspects then dominant in American faiths, Jonathan Edwards and Emerson may speak, the one for American Calvinism in its most intellectually rigorous form, the other for American transcendentalism in its most persuasive idiom. In any event, the impulse to assert symbolic identities between nature and its god was sufficiently universal for a young man to absorb anywhere. At no less a hallowed shrine than his mother's knee, Melville heard the Dutch Reformed Catechism proclaiming man could learn much of God through His created universe — "a most elegant book, wherein all creatures, great and small, are as so many characters leading us to contemplate the invisible things of God."[6]

The sober ecclesiastics at Dort were suitably cautious in the phrase "leading us to contemplate," but, so Perry Miller tells us, even the rigorous Edwards went much further in his thought. To him the "images" and "shadows" of the natural world were not merely useful for illustrations of divine truths; they were evidence of Truth itself.[7] Yet even as Edwards accommodated Locke's psychology of sensation to a rearticulated Calvinism, Hume was carrying Locke's ideas to their logical conclusion. On such a basis, he demonstrated, there was no necessary correspondence between

---

[5]Book Third, Chapter III, "Symbols"; or as in Book Second, Chapter IX, "The Everlasting Yea": "Or what is Nature? Ha! why do I not name thee God? Art not thou the 'Living Garment of God'?"

[6]William H. Gilman, *Melville's Early Life and 'Redburn'* (New York, 1951), p. 81.

[7]See Miller's edition, with introduction, of *Images, or Shadows of Divine Things*, by Jonathan Edwards (New Haven, 1948).

the sensory impression — the "image" — and the objective, external stimulus, between the symbolic construction with which our mind necessarily deals and the objective reality which such mental constructions are taken to represent.

The success of Hume's destruction of the certainty of knowledge, together with all its devastating implications for thought generally, including religious belief, eventually set off what has been called a mania for epistemological investigation. Emerson, like his English and German fellows, was deeply shaken by the Scotch Goliath. But in the end, like them, he was able to reassert a faith, a confidence in the reading of the world as a symbol of God, founded on a depth of *intuitive* conviction beyond — or, at any rate, not susceptible to — rational argumentation or criticism.

At the same time, Emerson went beyond Edwards in denying the tragic possibilities of human error and suffering. It was the easy, cheerful benevolence of transcendentalism in its shallower reaches, as well as the complacent assurance in the myth of the new world paralleling it, which prompted both Hawthorne's rare excursions into satire and Melville's scorn. Melville, with far more direct experience of the world than Emerson, had found few Edens in the forecastle.

Yet almost everywhere he turned after coming back from the South Pacific — in the scorn of the Duyckinck circle in New York, in the Boston of his new wife's family, in the Berkshires with the Hawthornes, the Holmeses, and other New Englanders — he met the Emersonian ferment. So, for example, after hearing the seer, Melville in an early letter once included Emerson in his praise of "all men who dive," though with strong reservations.[8] And it was the admiring Sophia Hawthorne who sent the restless young man off to the boudoir to "read Mr. Emerson's Essays in presence of our beautiful picture"![9]

For the increasingly scornful Melville (as in *Pierre*, Bk. XIV, Chap. ii), writers like Emerson or Goethe or Carlyle quickly became that "guild of self-impostors, with a preposterous rabble of Muggletonian Scots and Yankees, whose vile brogue still the more bestreaks the stripedness of their Greek or German Neoplatonical originals." His own "ontological heroics," of which he writes so often to

---

[8] To Evert A. Duyckinck, 3 March 1849, *The Letters of Herman Melville*, ed. Merrell R. Davis, and William H. Gilman (New Haven, 1960), p. 79.

[9] From a letter to her mother, Autumn, 1850, quoted by Eleanor Melville Metcalf, *Herman Melville: Cycle and Epicycle* (Cambridge, Mass., 1953), p. 91.

Hawthorne in 1850-1851 while the whale was in his flurry, pursue the same questions of the nature of reality, the nature and existence of God, from a profoundly different vantage.

It would be absurd, of course, to make of *Moby-Dick* a systematic, discursive rebuttal of either Emersonian or more traditional ontological assumptions. Nonetheless, the represented experience of the novel is precisely that of the millennially old tradition viewed in a terrifying new perspective, of sensing faith and conviction disintegrate, so to speak, before one's eyes. We speak often, and with singular aptness, of the novel in metaphors of hunting, of questing, of going out to sea to "see"; what is seen and felt, what is projected here is that experience.

In Edwards and Emerson alike, the verb "see," once noticed, seems everywhere. It is another commonplace that the discoveries of optics and the investigations of color and light revolutionized men's way of looking at and thinking about the world. Yet what Edwards and even more Emerson "saw" they felt as reassurance about God's world. For Emerson, self-described as a "transparent eyeball," the apparent faults of the world lay not in the reality, but in our own imperfect vision. Life itself is an "angle of vision" and "man is measured by the angle at which he looks at objects." In *Nature* he disposes of evil and ugliness with the facility of a Shaftesbury or Pope: "The ruin or the blank that we see when we look at nature, is in our own eye"; "The Poet" finds that "the evils of the world are such only to the evil eye." But with Melville, when he later bought his own copy of the *Essays*, such passages provoked exasperated marginal comments. As against the bland pronouncement in "Spiritual Laws," "The good, compared to the evil which he sees, is as his own good to his own evil," Melville noted scathingly, "A perfectly good being, therefore, would see no evil.— But what did Christ see?— He saw what made him weep. . . ."[10]

In the novel much of the hunt, of course, is after fair but much-pursued and slighter game like Biblical literalism, theological hair-splitting and apologetics, or practice versus preaching. The Biblical accounts of Jonah or Job, for example, are old familiar targets, and Melville is neither particularly original nor always at his best in heavy-handed irony and jocularity. Neither is this delighted hatchet-work altogether to the point, dealing as it does only with the engrafted fruit, not the roots of conviction.

---

[10]Cited in William Braswell, "Melville as a Critic of Emerson," *American Literature*, IX (1937), 317-334; see p. 330.

The real triumph of the novel, both intellectually and esthetically, lies elsewhere; boldly, Melville adopted a symbolist esthetic —of the kind Emerson proclaimed in *Nature*— to express a vision of experience, with, at the same time, the profoundest questioning of its metaphysical premises. With a fuller sense of the radically symbolic quality of the mind's activity than any artist before him (Coleridge excepted), Melville created a great man tragically destroying himself because he assents fully and dogmatically to a symbolic interpretation of experience. Melville designed the tragedy of Ahab, the art of *Moby-Dick,* from material made to question the very foundation of that art.

It is the triumph of the novel that, as Thoreau would require, every natural fact is so intensely viewed it "flowers in a truth," even as that truth is questioned. Not Emerson himself could ask for a closer attention to the immediate, the familiar, the homely as the novel transmutes the grubby, greasy business of whaling into tragedy. But Emerson, in his determined effort to confront the divinity in the universe, had characteristically laid down the basis for his faith in a celebration of rural, pastoral nature. Melville, when he sent his searchers out to sea, confronted them with a nature vastly different. If, according to the young Thoreau,[11] "Nature will bear the closest inspection"—because, according to Emerson, nature is "the present expositor of the divine mind"—we can suppose Melville sending his seekers out to widen their angle of vision, not by the dimension of a study window in Concord (or Northampton)—but from Ishmael's forecastle.

So it is that the pervasive and persistently evoked juxtaposition of the land and the sea, together with the action of hunting, of seeking, fuse in the most important structural metaphor of the novel. But it is a metaphor premised on observations, leading to conclusions far different from Emerson's or Edwards'. Edwards, indeed, or any Puritan, was by no means unaware of the vile or the terrible, but his convictions about Divine Providence and corrupted man led him unwaveringly to connect the beautiful and the awe-inspiring with the former, the repellent with the latter. It follows, then, that while bowels and dung are attributes of filthy man, waterspouts or thunder are "shadows" of divine majesty and wrath, even as the beauty of the rural Connecticut valley "consists wholly of sweet mutual consents . . . with the supreme being." So much the

---

[11]i. e., in "A Natural History of Massachusetts" (1842).

more with Emerson, "Therefore is nature glorious with form, color, and motion" to hint or thunder to man the divine laws.[12]

But life as Melville had seen it had not been bounded by the angle the horizon made with the Connecticut and Musketaquid Rivers. When Emerson announced that the poet "disposes very easily of the most disagreeable facts," the fatuity of the remark prompted Melville's ironic "So it would seem. In this sense, Mr. E. is a great poet."[13] The *Pequod's* search, far from disposing of the disagreeable, is exactly the attempt to face those facts, to ponder their significance. The land, with its comfortable securities, is kept only at the price of received opinion, of taking a part for the whole of experience, of seeing with too narrow an angle of vision. As in the familiar apostrophe concluding the abrupt dismissal of Bulkington,

> "All deep, earnest thinking is but the intrepid effort of the soul to keep the open independence of her sea; while the wildest winds of heaven and earth conspire to cast her on the treacherous, slavish shore. . . . as in landlessness alone resides the highest truth, shoreless, indefinite as God — so, better is it to perish in that howling infinite, than be ingloriously dashed upon the lee, even if that were safety!" (Chap. XXIII, "The Lee Shore")

Whatever we take the whale and all its like to represent, this going out to "see" is the real "Honor and Glory of Whaling," as one chapter is called. The true whale hunter seeks the living, spouting whale, impatient with the stuffed and dessicated specimens, the inaccurate and misleading pictures offered ashore as representative reality. So it is, too, in the search for illumination, only the whale hunter "burns . . . the purest of oil, in its unmanufactured, and, therefore, unvitiated state . . . He goes and hunts for his oil, so as to be sure of its freshness and genuineness . . ." (Chap. XCVII, "The Lamp").

This enforces one of the postulates of the whale hunt — an endless process of hunt, capture, rendering, and hunting again. The other is: "To grope down into the bottom of the sea after them; to have one's hands among the unspeakable foundations, ribs, and very pelvis of the world; this is a fearful thing" (Chap. XXXII, "Cetology"). But wearying or terrifying, only in the search, in the

---

[12]Edwards, "The Beauty of the World," in *Images, or Shadows*, p. 135; Emerson, *Nature*, "Discipline."
[13]Braswell, p. 324.

unremitting, unblinking effort to face the disagreeable facts does manhood realize itself.

To go to sea, to dive more deeply, to enlarge the vision — what is it then that one sees? The Psalmist, St. Paul, the Bishops, Edwards, or Emerson found the revelation of a just divinity. In the novel we approach an immediate tactic (though not the grand strategy) in Queequeg's exclamation of outraged pain when the jaws of a dead shark reflexively snap on his hand. "Queequeg no care what god made him shark . . . wedder Fejee god or Nantucket god; but de god wat made shark must be one dam Ingin" (Chap. LXVI, "The Shark Massacre"). The very first "Extract," with multiple appropriateness from Genesis, reminds us that "God created great whales," and though we are genially warned not to take all "higgledy-piggledy whale statements" for "veritable gospel," we are all the same confronted immediately with the classic logic of the syllogism: The creation, we have the highest assurance, manifests the Creator; but this creation is notorius for its suffering, its indifferent injustice, its ruthless energy and merciless, predatory nature; therefore, such must be its Creator.

Now this outraged conclusion is everywhere forced on our attention in the novel — by Ahab. But properly to assess *Melville's* strategy, we must constantly observe the way he handles the symbolizing mode of perception. The tradition of the symbolic connection between the creation and the creator, in all of its many versions, is also everywhere in question here, but most especially in its transcendental form. The strategic, the fundamental, issue is conveniently though whimsically joined in the mocking of the mast-head dreamer rapt in mystic communion. In an image which could have found an honored place in Emerson's "Oversoul," Ishmael derides such a latter-day Spinoza or Neoplatonist as he risks plunging to his destruction: "lulled into such an opium-like . . . reverie is this absent-minded youth by the blending cadence of waves with thoughts, that at last he loses his identity; takes the mystic ocean at his feet for the visible image of that deep, blue, bottomless soul, pervading mankind and nature . . ." (Chap. XXXV, "The Mast-Head"). Yet in embodying elusive thoughts in the dimly perceived, beautiful but elusive forms, the dreamer loses his grip; only self-annihilation waits in that mystic ocean.

All the same, it is by the full exploitation of the symbolizing mode of perception that conclusions far other than those entertained in Concord or Northampton are suggested. Persistently images of pastoral or domestic tranquility are juxtaposed against the hidden dreadfulness of the sea. So many and so varied they could not possibly be catalogued here, we can nevertheless see how they come to a crisis in those climactic last days, when all seductively each day is more wonderously lovely than the last, and even Ahab speaks wistfully of how "the airs [sic] smells now, as if it blew from a far-away meadow; they have been making hay somewhere under the slopes of the Andes, Starbuck, and the mowers are sleeping among the newmown hay." But for him to sleep is to "rust amid greenness; as last year's scythes flung down"; the simple rural implement becomes the sign of death; it was Moby Dick who "had reaped away Ahab's leg, as a mower a blade of grass in the field" (Chap. CXXXII, "The Symphony"; Chap. XLI, "Moby Dick").

"The Gilder" chapter describes one of these days when nature gilds the surface with enchantment, and even the wary hunter has a "land-like feeling towards the sea," regarding it as "so much flowery earth," a "rolling prairie" where play-wearied children might sleep in the vales, and men, like colts, might roll in new morning clover. But he who would argue benignity ought in conscience to look beneath the memories of clovered pastures beyond Concord and Walden.

> "Consider the subtleness of the sea; how its most dreaded creatures glide under water, unapparent for the most part, and treacherously hidden beneath the loveliest tints of azure. Consider also the devilish brilliance and beauty of many . . . species of sharks. Consider, once more, the universal cannibalism of the sea; all whose creatures prey upon each other, carrying on eternal war since the world began.
>
> Consider all this; and then turn to this green, gentle, and most docile earth; consider them both, the sea and the land; and do you not find a strange analogy to something in yourself?" (Chap. LVIII, "Brit")

No longer do we see, with William Cullen Bryant, only "Nature's everlasting smile." All easy symbolizing analogies must undergo a forcible revaluation. We must acknowledge the universal cannibalism in which sharks and men alike participate, and we begin to see, in a wider angle of vision, all that to which custom and convention on land had blindered us. Thoreau had travelled much in Concord, but a whaling ship was Ishmael's Yale College and his Harvard. The vision of remorseless voracity beneath the deceiving surface is the experience of all genuine hunters for the oil of illumination. This is what they have seen that makes *them* weep.

What Emerson would call the veils of Nature are to Ahab, as he calls them in the famous passage, walls, pasteboard masks, deceiving appearance through which he proposes to thrust at the inscrutable malice he sees sinewing it from behind. To this, then, has come for him the effort to confront the image of divinity in the universe. In the long chapter "Moby Dick" Melville shows how and why Ahab had come to invert the traditional symbolic identification. The rage of Ahab has been called "the challenge of a disillusioned transcendentalism, which is impatient with material surfaces, eager to probe as far beyond them as possible, and doubtful as to the results of such an exploration." [14] But we must understand such a statement in a way not originally intended. Ahab and Melville unquestionably find a piously interpreted connection between nature and deity no longer tenable; Ishmael and Melville are surely doubtful of any other certainty resulting from a sea-search, but we ignore the progressive thrust of the novel if we fail to recognize that whatever doubts Ahab may entertain at points, by the end he has acceded to a settled and violent conviction terribly but merely the reverse of the traditional.

We must see that however disillusioned Ahab is with the pious reading, however blasphemously Ahab has read *this* not so "elegant book" of nature, his method is precisely that of the catechism, his conclusion not less theocentric than any Edwards' or Emerson's. He, too, insists on the symbolic connection between man and god if only in the malice of destruction.

Terrifying, enraging as this conviction is, Ahab faces it with indomitable will. But beyond there is an even more terrifying possibility he will not face. Something of the sort Hawthorne tried to express in his notebook after seeing Michelangelo's "Three Fates" in Italy in 1858. "I remember . . . being struck . . . with the terrible, stern, passionless severity, neither loving us nor hating us, that characterizes these ugly old women. If they were angry, or had the least spite against human kind, it would render them the more tolerable." [15] This ultimate possibility we must understand if we are fully to comprehend Ahab's tragedy; for even in the remotest fastness of his isolated grandeur, he dares not entertain any proposition denying a vital connection with an intelligible god, be it only in malice if nothing else.

---

[14]Harry Levin, *The Power of Blackness* (New York, 1958), p. 218.
[15]*Passages from the French and Italian Note-Books* (Boston, 1871, 1889), pp. 300-301.

Without quibbling over the possible formal requirements of tragedy, we can agree that Melville has seen the tragic possibilities of lonely grandeur, in the personal and spiritual isolation implied in the anarchic, self-defining individualism of a deeply Protestant, equalitarian society. In evident ways he seeks to establish tragic stature for his uncommon, common man, democratically distinguished by no other title than captain. This shaggy, at one time simple Quaker with ponderous brain, who has meditated long in the dark watches of the sea, has suffered as a Lear has suffered from the world's injustice, has scorned with Byronic defiance, is torn as Prometheus was torn, has felt the agonies of a crucifixion. These associations pervasively extend the dramatic dimension of Ahab— yet equally imply the significant differences which mark the special nature of his self-destruction.

In no way do I mean to deprecate Ahab's commanding stature; he rightly defines his presence in the novel as he pronounces his epitaph, "Oh, now I feel my topmost greatness lies in my topmost grief." But the nature of his tragedy remains to be defined. Lear's imperious egoism is redeemed by his suffering, but those humanities which Ahab once possessed (according to Captain Peleg) are ruthlessly discarded. In the Corposants scene Ahab had challenged the powers, "Come in thy lowest form of love, and I will kneel and kiss thee" (Chap. CXIX, "The Candles"), but the devotion of the Fool-like Pip is put aside with iron determination. Like an anguished Manfred, Ahab feels a scornful superiority to a merely cautious, prudential morality, but far from feeling any monstrous guilt of his own, his madness acknowledges only what has been done—not by, but to him. Promethean in his titanic defiance, he nevertheless despises his inferiors, his deeper wound self-inflicted, his vulture self-created. If there is a crucifixion in his face, the marks of the nails he bears in his palms are his own; when he rejects the pleas of the *Rachel's* captain, it is to himself he arrogates the power of mercy— "may I forgive myself" (Chap. CXXVIII, "The Pequod Meets the Rachel").

In short, Ahab, though he has greatly dared beyond his land-bound contemporaries in confronting a monstrous vision of the universe, dared greatly in defying the malignant power so conceived, yet not less than his contemporaries ashore does he hold the creation to revolve egocentrically about himself. And in so doing, like them he has only imposed his own solipsistic conception upon that world—a conception which has in no way any greater warrant for its validity than that of the most egregiously complacent argument from design. Putatively, like Father Mapple, in seeking pilot of a ship's world, he is even more like Father Mapple in being essentially convinced of his truth before he begins; Ahab seeks not to discover what may be truth, but to prove his truth.

What this means in defining Ahab's tragedy, and how we are led to see his position as tragic, can be clarified by reconsidering the effect of Hume's ideas. Jonathan Edwards did not need to question his conviction that the perceived world was charged with intelligible significance, but Emerson could achieve the peace of his covenant only after wrestling with the demon spectres convoked by the Scotch Goliath. He had at last to accommodate the new epistemology by identifying the creating mind of man with Providential purpose. Even as he discusses the "noble doubt" in *Nature*, Emerson adds, "It is a sufficient account of that Appearance we call the World, that God will teach a human mind . . . Whether nature enjoy a substantial existence without, or is only in the apocalypse of the mind, it is alike useful . . . to me." The assurance in this waiver is founded on the prior conviction, the "relation between the mind and matter is not fancied by some poet, but stands in the will of God . . ." Or as his contemporary journal adds, "The self of self creates the world through you." If by the 1840's, further experience had dampened this "Saturnalia of faith," he was still ready to describe "The Transcendentalist": "His thought — that is the Universe. . . . I — this thought which is called I — is the mould into which the world is poured like melted wax. The mould is invisible, but the world betrays the shape of the mould."[16]

Carlyle's "The Universe is but one vast symbol of God" or Emerson's equivalent "Nature is the symbol of spirit" assert, in effect, that the object and its significance are one. But for a mind not sharing the conviction of the radical correspondence of mind, matter, and God, such an epistemology must surely open appalling vistas. For if knowledge of the object may be merely illusion, then the avowed significance may be the wildest self-delusion. As Pierre will discover grimly not a year later, "Nature is not so much her own ever-sweet interpreter, as the mere supplier of that cunning alphabet, whereby selecting and combining as he pleases, each man reads his own peculiar lesson according to his own peculiar mind and mood" (Bk. XXV, Chap. iv). This, at last, is the "metaphys-

---

[16]*Nature*, Section VI, "Idealism"; Section IV, "Language"; journal entry for July 30, 1836, *Journals of Ralph Waldo Emerson* (ed. E. W. Emerson and W. E. Forbes, Boston, 1910), IV, 78; "The Transcendentalist" as a lecture was given in the winter of 1841-1842.

ical terror" contemplated by Ishmael, surpassing even Ahab's conviction in its fatal implications for the religious sensibility.

It is from this point of view, then, that Ahab may be considered
as a re-viewed figure of the Emersonian, self-reliant, self-creating,
self-destroying man, whose image of the "world betrays the shape
of the mould."

We are not questioning the heroic nature of the sea-faring
searcher, profundly distrusting the half-known truths of the land,
be they Calvinist or transcendental. Yet not only is meditation
wedded to the sea — there is the still deeper meaning of Narcissus
drowned attempting to grasp the tormenting image. "But that same
image, we ourselves see in all rivers and oceans. It is the image of
the ungraspable phantom of life; and this is the key to it all"
(Chap. I, "Loomings"). The image which Ahab saw in the world
is, finally, only what Narcissus saw — himself.

Modern psychological analysis of religious expression has famil-
iarized us with the sense in which Calvins and Luthers transformed
self-hates and guilts in their conceptions of deity. A hundred years
ago Melville here creates the meaning of an equivalent insight. As
the Calvinist finds wrathful justice in his ideas of the divine, as an
Emerson finds his aspirations to benevolent serenity matched in the
Concord landscape, so Ahab finds only his own hate and vengeful
desire in what he takes to be the malice of the whale. He, like the
rest in the action conjugated by Pip, "I look, you look," peers into
the mirror of the doubloon nailed to the mast and discovers that
"this round gold is but the image of the rounder globe, which, like
a magician's glass, to each and every man in turn but mirrors back
his own mysterious self" (Chap. XCIX, "The Doubloon").

Without gainsaying the cannibalism, the voracious horror which
lurks beneath the gilded surface, we come to see how Ahab has even
so but imputed his own hate and range into the inscrutable white
face. The assertion of malevolent *intelligence* and *motivation* makes
the same enormous leap into pure faith the orthodox and the transcendentalist have made. Ahab's "image" or "picture" of the whale
has ultimately no more authenticity than the erroneous pictures
found in incompetent books of "whale" lore, literally or metaphor-
ically considered. The mad zealot Gabriel finds the incarnation of
the Shaker God with as much or little warrant as Ahab. Ahab is destroyed—to this degree like his Biblical namesake—by establishing
false idols of his own making. Ahab, who may long ago have begun
by searching for meaning and truth, has finally only succeeded, as
Ishmael sees at length, in inverting delusion.

Only rarely these days is the piety of Father Mapple or Starbuck offered as a commentary on Ahab's blasphemy, and yet in a paradoxical way, each illuminates the others. Each of them in his own way, with less or greater desperation, asserts his kind of faith in the face of the measureless immensity confronting the sea-searcher. For Father Mapple it is the austere Old Testament moral of Job: "Though he slay me, yet will I trust him." Ahab makes not less a confession of faith in the thorough-going inversion, "I will maintain my own ways before him: Though he slay me, yet will I defy him still." Starbuck recites his tormented creed in the notable "Gilder" chapter. Faithful as Starbuck is, Ishmael finds his angle of vision insufficient, his judgment of Ahab too simplistic, his faith self-deception. His unaided virtue, founded on such an inadequate faith, cannot stand before the wrath of Ahab's more awful conviction. Justified not only morally but legally (a point repeatedly made) in wresting command from Ahab, he can only skulk impotently with a gun outside a closed door. Like his contemporary Tennyson, Starbuck has looked on "Nature, red in tooth and claw," but his only recourse is similarly a desperate reaffirmation of the old piety. On that day of "The Gilder," with all its ambivalently transcendental evocation of pastoral tranquility, Starbuck looks deep into the water but murmurs, "Loveliness unfathomable . . . Tell me not of thy teeth-tiered sharks, and thy kidnapping cannibal ways. Let faith oust fact, let fancy oust memory; I look deep down and do believe" (Chap. CXIV).

In comparison to this, Ahab is the deeper diver because he has faced the sharks, the cannibal ways. Yet the tragic perspective Melville provides through Ishmael leads us to see not only the inadequacy of Starbuck, but finally even of Ahab. Not because he is defeated and destroyed by powers far greater, a spectacle of awe or perhaps only pathos; not because he blasphemed, which merely distresses piety; but because he agreed there was a reality which made blasphemy meaningful. Not less than Starbuck or Father Mapple has he made a supreme assertion of faith, however much transposed his terms. Not less than they has he closed off the question, set the terms of the "search" before it even began, however more comprehensively. He seeks — no longer in open-minded search for whatever truth — but to wreak revenge in response to settled conviction.

The whale, like his vulture, is "the very creature he creates"; he himself drives the nails in his palms, he himself strings the gallows hemp for the hanging enigmatically prophesied by Fedallah. With

an eloquence and imagery Emerson would have fancied, Ahab de-
clares, "O Nature, and O soul of man! how far beyond all utterance
are your linked analogies; not the smallest atom stirs or lives on
matter, but has its cunning duplicate in mind" (Chap. LXX, "The
Sphynx"). To the end he proclaims the personal significance of the
universal riddle.

That we see both the magnificence and the peculiarly tragic nature of Ahab's "faith" is due, of course, to the angle of vision which
Ishmael supplies. Once Ishmael, like the others, was caught up in
the terrible grandeur of Ahab's vision. Once he, too, though with far
more dubiety, could assert the "linked analogies"—"some certain
significance lurks in all things, else all things are little worth, and
the round world itself but an empty cipher . . ." (Chap. XCIX, "The
Doubloon"). But the more Ishmael employs the analogical mode of
perception, the more aware he becomes of its fatal deceptions.

For if, in a simple inversion of the orthodox view of reality, Ahab
has made over the whale into an embodiment of all evil and malevolent purpose in the universe, Moby Dick comes eventually to suggest something quite different to Ishmael, implications far other
than those traditionally associated with color and light. The re-
fracted colors of the new optics were to Edwards not only a source
of beauty but "types," images and shadows of the divine, signs of
truth itself. For Emerson, somewhat less intoxicated by the time he
came to write "Experience," the discoveries of optics now became
an epistemological version of the Fall. "We have learned that we do
not see directly, but mediately, and that we have no means of cor-
recting these colored and distorting lenses which we are, or of com-
puting the amount of their errors. Perhaps these subject-lenses
have a creative power; perhaps there are no objects." But the old
faith reasserts itself: "The great and crescive self, rooted in absolute nature, supplants all relative existence . . . yet is the God the
native of these bleak rocks."

Such assurance was impossible for Ishmael. "It was the whiteness
of the whale that above all things appalled me." By a masterly
balancing of image against image, Melville defines Ishmael's growing awareness of the desperate possibility of a universe simply
meaningless, where all comforting analogies are only self-deceits.
Not even malevolent, which would at least be personal, in some
ways humanly apprehensible, but simply purposeless. Here is the
dubiety in full consciousness—"all things *are* little worth, and the
round world itself but an empty cipher," a Newtonian cryptogram
without meaning, an empty zero.

We cannot fail to recognize in this chapter Melville's representation of Hume's implications; the dialectic of the material moves inexorably to the probable conclusion: all we can know, finally, of all the baffling phenomena presented by some possibly objective world is sheer illusion, a symbolic construct only of our own minds. From this appalling angle Ishmael must deny the certain validity of any "argument from design," orthodox, transcendental, or Satanic.

To affirm that either Edwards' or Emerson's God was still "the native of these bleak rocks" now seems to Ishmael a Laplandish superstition, as if one were looking at, seeing a very probably colorless world through deifying glasses. In one astonishing passage he sums up the implications of epistemological investigation from Locke to Hume:

> ". . . is it, that as in essence whiteness is not so much a color as the visible absence of color, and at the same time the concrete of all colors . . . when we consider that other theory of the natural philosophers, that all other earthly hues — every stately or lovely emblazoning — the sweet tinges of the sunset skies and woods; yea, and the gilded velvets of butterflies, and the butterfly cheeks of young girls; all these are but subtle deceits, not actually inherent in substances, but only laid on from without; so that all deified Nature absolutely paints like the harlot, whose allurements cover nothing but the charnel-house within; and when we proceed further, and consider that the mystical cosmetic which produces every one of her hues, the great principle of light, for ever remains white or colorless in itself, and if operating without medium upon matter, would touch all objects, even tulips and roses, with its own blank tinge — pondering all this, the palsied universe lies before us a leper; and like wilful travellers in Lapland, who refuse to wear colored and coloring glasses upon their eyes, so the wretched infidel gazes himself blind at the monumental white shroud that wraps all the prospect around him. And of all these things the Albino whale was the symbol."
> (Chap. XLII, "The Whiteness of the Whale")

Pointedly, the two chapters — "Moby Dick" for Ahab, "The Whiteness of the Whale" for Ishmael — are paired, barely one third of the way through the novel. The remainder of the novel takes all its significance from this differentiation. Now constantly borne in upon our attention, defining and shaping the impact of the novel upon our consciousness, are not only all those many images ambivalently linking pastoral tranquility and horror, but all the many overt statements, all the many images which point to a world

neither benevolent nor malevolent, just icily, glacially cold, impersonal, indifferent, purposeless, meaningless.

The fire imagery of the novel has had long scrutiny, but it is
rarely observed how images of ice and glacial coldness play their
subtle counterpart. If Ahab's harpoon is forged in the blue-hot
flame of Perth's fire, the barbs nevertheless are to be made "sharp
as the needle-sleet of the Icy Sea." In all the iron cold that invests
New England, only man is "the one warm spark in the heart of an
arctic crystal." The "heartless immensities" in which Pip was lost
are the counterpart of the "heartless voids and immensities of the
universe." Not even Moby Dick will escape the "horrible vulturism
of earth! from which not the mightiest whale is free." The sea in-
differently bears up or shatters both whales and ships; it is a "fiend
to its own offspring . . . Like a savage tigress that tossing in the
jungle overlays her own cubs, so the sea dashes even the mightiest
whales against the rocks, and leaves them there side by side with
the split wrecks of ships. No mercy, no power but its own controls
it. Panting and snorting like a mad battle steed that has lost its
rider, the masterless ocean overruns the globe" (Chap. LVIII,
"Brit").

The certainty of purposelessness is, by the very premises on
which such an idea is advanced, impossible; but the appalling
thought forces increasing attention. Beyond the veil, behind the
mask, beneath the inscrutable whiteness may be—nothing. This is
the terror which Ahab will not, at least for long, contemplate; but
this is what the search for the white whale comes to signify for
Ishmael. He had begun with the knowledge that to "have one's
hands among the unspeakable foundations, ribs, and very pelvis of
the world; this is a fearful thing." When he is at last among the
ribs and pelvis of the skeleton in the Arsacides, he finds only —
death. "I saw no living thing within; naught was there but bones"
(Chap VII, "A Bower in The Arsacides"). With an equally grim
jocularity, he finds he cannot make out the back parts, still less
"how understand his head? much more, how comprehend his face,
when face he has none?" (Chap. LXXXVI, "The Tail").

With neither face nor voice, the universe Ishmael ultimately confronts is neither benevolent nor yet malevolent, with neither evident meaning nor purpose. Still, just as the traditionally supposed
Solomon of Ecclesiastes found, it is sufficiently clear that in this
world, sorrow outweighs joy, pain and anguish and indifferent destruction are more faithful indicators than happiness. In spite of
spring grasses and blue skies, Ishmael must acknowledge, like

Bartleby facing the dead blank walls of The Tombs, "I know where I am." Of only two things can man be reasonably certain, and one is: This world was *not* made for his delight, not even his discipline and punishment.

With Ishmael's angle of vision Melville creates an insight transcending, then, not only Father Mapple or Starbuck, but, most signally, Ahab. It is a view uncommitted to any dogmas, neither positively nor negatively theocentric; a view tentative and considerate of alternatives; one that seeks justly to evaluate and arrive at a sanely stable (if constantly provisional) understanding of the "truth of experience." "What plays the mischief with the truth," Melville wrote to Hawthorne late that memorable spring, "is that men will insist upon the universal application of a temporary feeling or opinion."[17]

Without at all displacing Ahab as the dramatic center of the novel—in some sense of that slippery word, as "hero"—Ishmael develops a moral center and defining force, somewhat erratically, doubtless, in Melville's handling, and unsystematically, but nevertheless the indispensable perspective. It is shaped by the recognition at once of the "absurdity" of man's position in a purposeless universe, and yet the sober insistence, since this is all there is, there we must somehow make a life for ourselves. This is the other certainty.

In a possibly meaningless world, where man is all too probably an inconsequential accident, he *is* alive and somehow defined. Hume undermined the notion that we can perceive even self as an objective entity, but at least, to be human is, precisely, to be aware of being human. One of the most insistently presented patterns in Ahab's tragic development is his progressive, wilful isolation from humanity and humane values. In defining contrast to this, again, is Ishmael's turning from his defiantly whimsical outcast mood to Queequeg. Between them grows what may inadequately be termed a "communion," undoctrinaire, based on no reference external to itself, transcending all differences of color, race, language, and nominal creed, not as sons of God, but as men. Queequeg's humanity, generosity and selflessness can exist irrespective of any institutionalized ethic, and despite the otherwise all too evident predatory nature of the world.

To be sure, this communion is represented perhaps rather too elaborately in the self-conscious analogy of the monkey-rope, rather

---

[17]Letter of 1 [?] June 1851; *Letters,* p. 131.

too graphically in the symbolic marriage at the Spouter Inn. Yet they together, Ishmael and Queequeg, shielded from the petrifying cold, are the "one warm spark in the heart of an arctic crystal." This is doubless not an answer to the human predicament, but it is a necessary condition of existence. In one of its aspects it is passional love, just as the mating whales make the still center in the heart of the tornado of the Grand Armada. In its more general aspect it engages that the open independence of the sea and human interdependence, the never-ending self-reliant search and the concomitant responsibility of human love need not and must not be mutually exclusive. Against the weight of this moral center, Ahab is weighed, measured, and found wanting.

The tragic power of Ahab is the power of America's deepest cultural commitment, to the figure of the isolated, self-reliant individual, defining himself against both society and nature. The power of the novel is in the encompassing vision transcending this. What emerges is not a pious orthodoxy of belief and humility, nor yet solely the grandeur of Ahab's defiance, but a dynamic, unresolved tension between an experienced meaninglessness and the stubborn will to find meaning in experience, between the lonely grandeur of the lonely individual soul and the rights of human love. There is no *answer* here, only a vision of the conditions for the never-ending search in which mankind must forever engage — in the new world not less than in the old. Eden is not here, nor anywhere, but must forever be sought, worked for, with all of man's best energies and all his highest hopes, in all humility and in all the meaning of his humanity.

Here Melville has been beyond both piety and despair—not to some new cosmic moral revelation — but to the sobering proposition: If there is to be a moral order at all in this world, man—weak, flawed, fallible as he is—must somehow forge it himself out of his own human experience.

Walter Bezanson

[Dynamic and Structure in *Moby-Dick*]

By the term "dynamic" I mean the action of forces on bodies at rest. The whaling matter in *Moby-Dick* is in no sense at rest, excepting as here or there occurs a failure in effect. For the most part the stuff and data of whaling are complexly subject to the action of a force which can be defined and illustrated. So too is the whole narrative base of the book, which is something far more than a record of what anyone aboard the *Pequod* would agree had happened. There is a dynamic operating on both matter and narrative which distinguishes *Moby-Dick* from logs, journals, and histories.

One of two forces, or their combination, is commonly assumed to provide the dynamic of *Moby-Dick*. The first, of course, is Captain Ahab, the dark protagonist, the maimed king of the quarter-deck whose monomania flows out through the ship until it drowns his men — mind and (finally) body. That he is the dominant "character" and the source of "action" seems obvious. The reader's image of him is a lasting one. Is Ahab the dynamic?

From "*Moby-Dick:* Work of Art," *Moby-Dick Centennial Essays*, ed. Tyrus Hillway and Luther S. Mansfield (Dallas: Southern Methodist University Press, 1953), pp. 35-57.

The alternative force, it is commonly assumed, is Moby Dick himself, that particular white "spouting fish with a horizontal tail" about whom legend and murmured lore have woven enchantments, so that he looms a massive phantom in the restless dreams of the *Pequod's* captain and crew. His name gives the novel its title. He is prime antagonist of the tale. Is Moby Dick the dynamic?

Both these interpretations have their uses, especially when taken together in a subject-predicate relation. But there is a third point of view from which neither Ahab nor the White Whale is the central dynamic, and I find it both compelling and rewarding, once recognized. This story, this fiction, is not so much about Ahab or the White Whale as it is about Ishmael, and I propose that it is he who is the real center of meaning and the defining force of the novel.

The point becomes clearer when one realizes that in *Moby-Dick* there are two Ishmaels, not one. The first Ishmael is the enfolding sensibility of the novel, the hand that writes the tale, the imagination through which all matters of the book pass. He is the narrator. But who then is the other Ishmael? The second Ishmael is not the narrator, not the informing presence, but is the young man of whom, among others, narrator Ishmael tells us in his story. He is simply one of the characters in the novel, though to be sure a major one whose significance is possibly next to Ahab's. This is forecastle Ishmael or the younger Ishmael of "some years ago." There is no question here of dual personality or *alter ego*, such as really exists, for instance, in Poe's "William Wilson" or Conrad's "The Secret Sharer." Narrator Ishmael is merely young Ishmael grown older. He is the man who has already experienced all that we watch forecastle Ishmael going through as the story is told.

The distinction can be rendered visual by imagining, for a moment, a film version of the novel. As the screen lights up and the music drops to an obbligato we look on the face of narrator Ishmael (a most marvelous face, I should judge), and the magic intonation begins:

> Call me Ishmael. Some years ago—never mind how long precisely —having little or no money in my purse, and nothing particular to interest me on shore, I thought I would sail about a little and see the watery part of the world. It is a way of driving off the spleen, and regulating the circulation. Whenever I find myself . . .

And as the cadenced voice goes on, the face of the Ishmael who has a tale to tell fades out, the music takes up a brisk piping air, and whom should we see tripping along the cobbled streets of New Bedford, carpetbag in hand, but forecastle Ishmael. It is a cold winter's night, and this lonely young man is in search of lodgings. For very soon now he plans to go a-whaling.

Meanwhile we hear the voice, always the magic voice, not of the boy we watch with our eyes, but of one who long since went aboard the *Pequod*, was buried in the sea and resurrected from it. This voice recounts the coming adventures of young Ishmael as a story already fully experienced. Experienced, but not fully understood; for as he explicitly says: "It was the whiteness of the whale that above all things appalled me. But how can I hope to explain myself here; and yet, in some dim, random way, explain myself I must, else all these chapters might be naught." So we are reminded by shifts of tense from time to time that while forecastle Ishmael is busy hunting whales narrator Ishmael is sifting memory and imagination in search of the many meanings of the dark adventure he has experienced. So deeply are we under the spell of the narrator's voice that when at last the final incantation begins — " 'And I only am escaped alone to tell thee'. . . . The drama's done. . . ." — then at last, as forecastle Ishmael floats out of the *Pequod's* vortex, saved, we look again on the face of Ishmael narrator. And we realize that for many hours he has been sitting there and has never once moved, except at the lips; sitting in profound reverie, yet talking, trying to explain "in some dim, random way" what happened, for "explain myself I must."

The distinction between the function of the two Ishmaels is clear. Yet it would be a mistake to separate them too far in temperament. Certainly young Ishmael is no common sailor thoughtlessly enacting whatever the fates throw his way. He is a pondering young man of strong imagination and complex temperament; he will, as it were, become the narrator in due time. But right now he is aboard the *Pequod* doing his whaleman's work and trying to survive the spell of Ahab's power. The narrator, having survived, is at his desk trying to explain himself to himself and to whoever will listen. The primary use of the distinction is to bring the narrator forward as the essential sensibility in terms of which all characters and events of the fiction are conceived and evaluated. The story is his. What, then, are some of his primary commitments of mind and imagination as he shapes his story through one hundred and thirty-five chapters?

As a lover of laughter and hilarity, Ishmael delights in the incongruities. Of whales, for instance: whales spout steam because they think so much; they have no nose, but don't really need one—

there are no violets in the sea; they are very healthy, and this is because they get so much exercise and are always out of doors, though rarely in the fresh air; and they like to breakfast on "sailor tarts, that is whaleboats full of mariners." Ishmael has too a deep belly laugh for the crudities and obscenities that mark the life of animal man, making much more than is proper of some talk about gentlemen harpooning ladies, relishing a Rabelaisian remark about "head winds" versus "winds from astern," and penning a memorable canonization of a rarely discussed part of the anatomy in "The Cassock." But as a purveyor of the "genial, desperado philosophy," his most characteristic humor is that of the hyena laugh: he begins his tale with a mock confession of suicidal impulses; he sends young Ishmael running to his bunk after his first encounter with a whale to make out his will; he reports that some sailors are so neat they wouldn't think of drowning "without first washing their faces"; and he delights in Queequeg's solemn decision, when he seems mortally ill, whereby the good savage suddenly "recalled a little duty ashore, which he was leaving undone; and therefore . . . changed his mind about dying." Beneath Ishmael's mask of hypochondria is the healthy grimace of a man who stands braced to accept "the universal thump" and to call out: "Who ain't a slave?" To Ishmael "a good laugh is a mighty good thing, and rather too scarce a good thing; the more's the pity."

As narrator Ishmael betrays a passion for all faraway places and things, "Patagonian sights and sounds," imagined cities, fabled heroes, the sepulchers of kings. His rich imagination is stirred by all that is secret, mysterious, and undecipherable in the great riddles of mankind. He both cherishes and mocks the great systems of the philosophers, the operations of "chance, free will, and necessity," the great religions and heresies of the past. His fascination with ancient lore and wisdom runs from Adam to Zoroaster; to help him tell his tale he marshals the great mythic figures of past centuries and all black-letter commentaries thereon.

His temperament is complex. If one of its facets, that of the "Sub-Sub-Librarian," has an antiquarian glint, another glows with the love of action. Each cry from the masthead alerts him from dreamy speculations to the zest of the hunt. Every lowering away starts his blood pounding. He is a superb narrator of the frenzied strivings of the boat crew as they press in for the kill, chanting their terror and competence as they enter "the charmed, churned circle" of eternity. When the death-deed is done, when the whirl slowly widens, he takes up the song of dismemberment. For the weapons of the chase, the red tools of slaughter, the facts of procedure, he

has an insatiable curiosity. Cutting in, trying out, stowing down —
the whole butcher-slab routine of processing the dead whale he en-
dows with ritual certainty, transforming dirty jobs into acts of ceremonial dignity. Ishmael's voice translates the laughter and wild
deeds of the bloody crew into the ordered rites of primitive tribal
priests.

Narrator Ishmael has an instinct for the morally and psycholog-
ically intricate. He presses close in after the intertwinings of good
and evil, tracks down the baffling crisscross of events and ideas,
ponders their ambiguities and inversions. He is keen for a paradox
and quick to see polarities—so keen in fact that the whole experience seems a double vision of what is at once noble and vile, of all
that is lovely and appalling. This two-fold sensitivity marks his
probings into the life-images of those he has known — whether in
his grand-scale exposition of the "ungodly, god-like man, Captain
Ahab" or in the compassionate recollection of little Pip, for a time
lost overboard in the "heartless immensity" of the sea, and gone
divinely mad from it. Whether noting that Queequeg's tomahawk-
pipe "both brained his foes and soothed his soul" or contemplating
"the interlinked terrors and wonders of God," he turns the coin
both ways. He makes it a crisis of the first order that young Ishmael, both a brooder and a good companion, was drawn with the
rest of the crew by the dark magnetic pull of the captain's monomania, wavering between allegiance to that uncommon king—Ahab
—and to "the kingly commons"—the crew. Only the traumatic re-
vulsion on the night of "The Try-Works" saved young Ishmael—"a
strange (and ever since inexplicable) thing" which the narrator
now explains symbolically: "Give not thyself up, then, to fire, lest
it invert thee, deaden thee; as for the time it did me."

Above all one notes the narrator's inexhaustible sense of wonder.
Wonder at the wide Pacific world, with its eternal undulations;
wonder at the creatures of the deep; wonder at man — dreamer,
doer, doubter. To him in retrospect the whale has become a mighty
analogue of the world, of man, of God. He is in awe before the
whale: its massive bulk, tiny eyes, great mouth, white teeth; its
narrow throat and cavernous belly; the spout; the hump; the
massed buttress of its domed head; the incomparable power and
magic of its fanning, delicate tail. It is wonder that lies at the center of Ishmael's scale of articulation, and the gamut runs out either
way toward fear and worship.

Enough of evocation. Every reader of *Moby-Dick* can and will
want to enlarge and subtilize the multiple attributes of Ishmael.
The prime experience for the reader is the narrator's unfolding

sensibility. With it we have an energy center acting outward on the inert matter of nature and experience, releasing its possibilities for art. Whereas forecastle Ishmael drops in and out of the narrative with such abandon that at times a reader wonders if he has fallen overboard, the Ishmael voice is there every moment from the genesis of the fiction in "Call me Ishmael" to the final revelation of the "Epilogue" when "The drama's done." It is the narrator who creates the microcosm and sets the terms of discourse.

But this Ishmael is only Melville under another name, is he not? My suggestion is that we resist any one-to-one equation of Melville and Ishmael. Even the "Melville-Ishmael" phrase, which one encounters in critical discussions, though presumably granting a distinction between autobiography and fiction, would seem to be only a more insistent confusion of the point at stake unless the phrase is defined to mean either Melville or Ishmael, not both. For in the process of composition, even when the artist knowingly begins with his own experience, there are crucial interventions between the act that was experience and the re-enactment that is art — intrusions of time, of intention, and especially of form, to name only a few. Which parts of Ishmael's experience and sensibility coincide with Melville's of physical and psychological history and in just what ways is a question which is initially only tangential to discussion of *Moby-Dick* as a completed work of art.

But what of structure? That there is a dynamic excitation in *Moby-Dick* sympathetic readers have not denied. Is the effect of Ishmael's energy, then, simply to fling the matter in all directions, bombarding the reader with the accelerated particles of his own high-speed imagination? Is Ishmael's search for "some dim, random way" to explain himself not merely a characterization of the complexity of his task but also a confession of his inadequacy to find form? The questions are crucial, for although readers will presumably go on reading *Moby-Dick* whichever way they are answered, the critical reader will not be encouraged to keep coming back unless he can "see" and "feel" the tension of controlling forces.

To an extraordinary extent Ishmael's revelation of sensibility is controlled by rhetoric. Throughout the tale linguistic versatility and subtle rhythmic patterns exploit sound and sense with high calculation. Almost at random one chooses a sentence: "And ever, as the white moon shows her affrighted face from the steep gullies in the blackness overhead, aghast Jonah sees the rearing bowsprit pointing high upward, but soon beat downward again towards the tormented deep." It is a successful if traditional piece of incantation

with is rising and falling movements manipulated to bring a striking force on the qualitative word "aghast." Its mood is typically
Gothic-romantic (pictorial equivalents would be certain passages
from Poe or the sea-paintings of Ryder), but structurally its allegiance is to the spacious prose of the seventeenth century. Although
the passage is from Father Mapple's sermon, it is in no way un-
representative; there are scores of sentences throughout *Moby-Dick*
of equal or greater rhetorical interest.

Of the narrative's several levels of rhetoric the simplest is a relatively straightforward *expository* style characteristic of many passages scattered through the cetological accounts. But it is significant
that such passages are rarely sustained, and serve chiefly as transitions between more complex levels of expression. Thus a series of
expository sentences in the central paragraph of the chapter on
"Cutting In" comes to this point: "This done, a broad, semicircular
line is cut round the hole, the hook is inserted, and the main body
of the crew striking up a wild chorus, now commence heaving in one
dense crowd at the windlass." Whether it cannot or will not, Ishmael's sensibility does not endure for long so bare a diction: "When
instantly, the entire ship careens over on her side; every bolt in her
starts like the nail-heads of an old house in frosty weather; she
trembles, quivers, and nods her frighted mastheads to the sky."
The tension is maintained through a following sentence, strict exposition returns in the next, and the paragraph concludes with an
emotionally and grammatically complex sentence which begins with
exposition, rises to a powerful image of whale flesh hoisted aloft
where "the prodigious blood-dripping mass sways to and fro as if
let down from the sky," and concludes with a jest about getting
one's ears boxed unless he dodges the swing of the bloody mess.
Even in the rhetorically duller chapters of exposition it is a rare
paragraph over which heat lightning does not flicker.

A second level of rhetoric, the *poetic*, is well exemplified in Ahab's
soliloquy after the great scene on the quarter-deck. As Matthiessen
has shown, such a passage can easily be set as blank verse:

> I leave a white and turbid wake;
> Pale waters, paler cheeks, where'er I sail.
> The envious billows sidelong swell to whelm
> My track; let them; but first I pass.

Because the rhythms here play over abstract metrical pattern, as
in poetry, they are evenly controlled—too evenly perhaps for prose,
and the tone seems "literary."

Quite different in effect is a third level of rhetoric, the *idiomatic*. Like the poetic it occurs rather rarely in a pure form, but we have an instance in Stubb's rousing exordium to his crew:

> "Pull, pull, my fine hearts-alive; pull, my children; pull, my little ones . . . Why don't you break your backbones, my boys? . . . Easy, easy; don't be in a hurry—don't be in a hurry. Why don't you snap your oars, you rascals? Bite something, you dogs! . . ."

Here the beat of oars takes the place of the metronomic meter and allows more freedom. The passage is a kind of rowing song and hence is exceptional; yet it is related in tone and rhythm to numerous pieces of dialogue and sailor talk, especially to the consistently excellent idiom of both Stubb and young Ishmael.

One might venture a fourth level of rhetoric, the *composite*, simply to assure the inclusion of the narrator's prose at its very best. The composite is a magnificent blending of the expository, the poetic, the idiomatic, and whatever other elements tend to escape these crude categories:

> The Nantucketer, he alone resides and riots on the sea; he alone, in Bible language, goes down to it in ships; to and fro ploughing it as his own special plantation. *There* is his home; *there* lies his business, which a Noah's flood would not interrupt, though it overwhelmed all the millions in China. He lives on the sea, as prairie cocks in the prairie; he hides among the waves, he climbs them as chamois hunters climb the Alps. For years he knows not the land; so that when he comes to it at last, it smells like another world, more strangely than the moon would to an Earthsman. With the landless gull, that at sunset folds her wings and is rocked to sleep between billows; so at nightfall, the Nantucketer, out of sight of land, furls his sails, and lays him to his rest, while under his very pillow rush herds of walruses and whales.

The passage is a great one, blending high and low with a relaxed assurance; after shaking free from the literary constrictions of the opening lines, it comes grandly home. And how does it relate to event and character? Ishmael's memory of the arrival at Nantucket, a mere incident in the movement of the plot, is to Ishmael now an imaginative experience of high order; and this we must know if we are to know about Ishmael. The whole chapter, "Nantucket," is a prose poem in the barbaric jocular vein, and it is as valuable a part of the documentation of Ishmael's experience as are the great "scenes." It is less extraneous to the meaning of the book than are many of the more average passages about Captain Ahab. The same could be said for other great passages of rhetoric, such as the marvelous hymn to spiritual democracy midway in "Knights and Squires." The first level of structure in *Moby-Dick* is the interplay of pressure and control through extraordinarily high rhetorical effects.

Beneath the rhetoric, penetrating through it, and in a sense rising above it, is a play of symbolic forms which keeps the rhetoric from dropping into exercise or running off in pyrotechnics. The persistent tendency in *Moby-Dick* is for facts, events, and images to become symbols. Ahab makes the most outright pronouncement of the doctrine of correspondences on which such a tendency depends, and to which almost all characters in the book are committed: "O Nature, and O soul of man! how far beyond all utterance are your linked analogies! not the smallest atom stirs or lives on matter, but has its cunning duplicate in mind." No less sensitive to symbolic values than Ahab is the young Ishmael in the forecastle. It is he who unfolds moral analogues from the mat-making, from the monkey-rope, from squeezing the case. He resembles Ahab in his talent for taking situations "strongly and metaphysically."

So on down the roster of the crew, where symbols and superstitions blend. Can there be any doubt that it is above all the enfolding imagination of the narrator which sets and defines the symbolic mode that pervades the entire book? From the richly emblematic theme of "meditation and water" in the opening chapter, to the final bursting of the "black bubble" of the sea which releases young Ishmael, the narrator sets the symbolic as the primary mode of self-examination and communication. He is predisposed to see events, however incidental, as "the sign and symbol" of something larger. To Ishmael "some certain significance lurks in all things, else all things are little worth, and the round world itself but an empty cipher. . . ."

Most commonly the symbols begin with a generative object: a waif-pole, a coin, a compass needle, a right-whale's head. The symbolic events begin with a chance incident: the dropping of his speaking trumpet by the Captain of the *Goney* (the nameless future), finding ambergris in a blasted whale (unexpected sweetness at the core of corruption), the chasing of the *Pequod* by Malay pirates (the pursuer pursued). Both give the tale solidity, for the objects and events are objects and events before they become meanings. But all the symbols do not rise out of tangible referents. We have to take into account also the narrator's love for "a furious trope" which often far exceeds the simple metaphorical function of comparison; the thing to which analogy is made — a pyramid, an elephant, a Leyden jar, a bird, a mythic figure — may itself enter the circle of symbolic values through recurrent reference. Thus the imagery brings scope to the limited range of symbols available on board the *Pequod*. Whereas the object-symbols in a sense carry the "plot," elucidating the experience of young Ishmael, Ahab, the mates and crew (as well as serving the narrator), the image-symbols chiefly reveal the psyche of the narrator through images of procreation and animality, mechanization and monomania, enchantment and entombment.

Though simpler objects, events, or images may connote primarily some one thing, as a shark means rapacious evil, most symbols which Ishmael develops in his narration express a complex of meanings which cannot easily be reduced to paraphrase and are not finally stable in other than their own terms. So it is with the *Pequod* herself and the ships she passes, with the root metaphors of earth, air, fire, and water which proliferate so subtly; and so it is with the most dynamic word-image-symbol of the tale: "white" (or "whiteness"). Their meanings are not single but multiple; not precisely equatable but ambiguous; not more often reinforcing than contradictory. The symbolism in *Moby-Dick* is not static but is in motion; it is in process of creation for both narrator and reader. Value works back and forth: being extracted from objects, it descends into the consciousness; spiraling up from the consciousness, it envelops objects.

Symbolism is so marked a characteristic of the narrator's microcosm that it is possible to phrase Ahab's tragedy not only in moral, social, and psychological terms, but in "structural" terms as well. Clearly Ahab accepts the symbolic as a source of cognition and of ethics. It was a symbolic vision that brought him on his quest, as no one senses with stronger discomfort than Starbuck, who stands alone in his sturdy, limited world of facts and settled faith. Yet the tragedy of Ahab is not his great gift for symbolic perception, but his abandonment of it. Ahab increasingly reduces all pluralities to the singular. His unilateral reading of events and things becomes a narrow translation in the imperative mood. Unlike young Ishmael, who is his equal in sensitivity but his inferior in will and authority, Ahab walls off his receptiveness to the complexities of experience, replacing "could be" or "might be" with "must." His destruction follows when he substitutes an allegorical fixation for the world of symbolic potentialities.

Ishmael's predilection for keying his narrative in the symbolic mode suggests another aspect of structure. *Moby-Dick* lies close to the world of dreams. We find the narrator recalling at length a remembered dream of his childhood. Stubb attempts a long dream-analysis to Flask after he has been kicked by Ahab. It is not strange, then, that young Ishmael's moment of greatest crisis, the night of the try-works when he is at the helm, should be of a traumatic order. More subtly, numerous incidents of the narrative are bathed in a dream aura: the trancelike idyll of young Ishmael at the masthead, the hallucinatory vision of the spirit spout, the incredible appearance on board of the devil himself accompanied by "five dusky phantoms," and many others. The narrator's whole effort to communicate the timeless, spaceless concept of "The Whiteness of the Whale" is an act of dream analysis. "Whether it was a reality or a dream, I never could entirely settle," says the narrator of his childhood dream; and so it was with much of what occurred aboard the *Pequod*. Ishmael's tale is to be listened to in terms of a tradition that runs from Revelation to *Finnegan's Wake*. Dream sense is an important mood in *Moby-Dick*; and dream form, to the extent there is such a verbal form, is an incipient structural device of the book. At regular intervals the narrator, in his intense effort to explain himself, resorts to a brief passage in which there is a flashing concentration of symbols that hold for a moment and then disappear. It is a night device for rendering daytime experience, and in *Moby-Dick* it happens again and again.

Any rigorous definition of structure must lead us on to consider the nature and relation of the constituent parts. Since the tale is divided into "parts" by the narrator himself (135 chapters, plus prefatory materials and "Epilogue"), one cannot escape considering the extent to which individual chapters themselves are structural units. We shall have to pass over such chapters, probably the largest group, as are devoted to the movement of narrative or to character analysis; the form here falls in a general way within the customary patterns of novelistic structure. Two chapter forms, however, are sufficiently non-novelistic to invite comment, the first of these being the dramatic. The term "dramatic" is here used in a technical, not qualitative sense, and refers to such devices of the playwright's script as italicized stage directions, set speeches with the speaker named in capitals, straight soliloquies, and dialogue without commentary. More than a tenth of the chapters are in this sense dramatic, some ten having strictly dramatic form without narrative intrusion, and another half-dozen or so using some script devices along with the narrative. The most successful of the strict-form group is certainly "Midnight, Forecastle," a ballet-like scene which superbly objectifies the crew in drunken exultation over the quest. But the two greatest are in the second group. "The Quarter-Deck," Ishmael's curtain-raising treatment of the quest theme, is a triumph of unified structure, conceived with extreme firmness and precision of detail. The powerful dramatic structure of the chapter — prologue, antiphonal choral address, formal individual debate, and group ceremonial — is a superb invention on free-traditional lines, unhampered by stage techniques yet profiting from them. The other great dramatic scene, a counterpart to "The Quarter-Deck" both thematically and structurally, is the massive Ahab-and-his-crew scene late in the book, "The Candles." The chapter is not so firmly conceived as its forerunner; and this, rather than its subject matter, is what brings it dangerously close to seeming overwrought and a bit out of hand. The key to the structure here lies in the narrator's word "tableau," a dramatic device of considerable currency in nineteenth-century America. As the primary symbols of fire and whiteness melt hotly into each other for the first time, we see a series of memorable tableaux lit by storm lightning and corposant flames between "intervals of profound darkness." The piece is a series of blinding kaleidoscopic flashes which reveal the alarmed mates, the primitives in their full demonic strength, Ahab in a fury of ritual power. The "enchanted" crew, which near this same quarter-deck had made its jubilant pledge, now hangs from the rigging "like a knot of numbed wasps"; and when Ahab brandishes his burning harpoon among them (an unstated completion of the image), "the mariners did run from him in a terror of dismay." The two chapters, "The Quarter-Deck" and "The Candles," are twin centers of gravity in ordering the structure of the Ahab theme. The two fields of force are possibility and necessity, and Ahab's shift is from initial ecstasy to final frenetic compulsiveness.

A second unusual element of chapter structure in *Moby-Dick* grows out of the sermon form. Most famously there is Father Mapple's sermon (chapter ix), a piece of sustained eloquence in the idiomatic-composite style. From his *text* in Jonah the old sailor-preacher moves at once to two *doctrines* (the Christian pattern of sin and repentance, and the hardness of obeying God); enters a highly imaginative narrative *explication* of the Biblical story; comes next to *applications* and *uses* (that the congregation shall take Jonah as "a model for repentance" and the preacher shall "preach the Truth to the face of falsehood") and concludes with an *exhortation* (the very subtly constructed incantation on the double-themed coda of Woe and Delight). Somewhat buried away in another chapter, "Stubb's Supper," is the shorter sermon in which Fleece, the Negro cook, one night preaches to the sharks in a serio-comic vein. As he peers over the *Pequod's* side with his lantern at the murderous feasting down below, Fleece addresses his "congregation" first as "Fellow-critters," then as "Belubed fellow-critters," and finally as "Cussed fellow-critters," the final imprecation sharpening Fleece's ominous doctrine that "all angel is not'ing more dan de shark well goberned." The structural pattern, especially in its repetitive address, is clearly derived from the folk tradition of the Negro sermon.

These are not the only two "sermons" in *Moby-Dick*. Although the free essay tradition from Montaigne to Hazlitt provides a more comfortable prototype for the more loosely ordered speculative chapters, most of these have a prophetic or protestant vein that pulls them over toward the sermon tradition. Again and again throughout the narrative a chapter comes to its climax in a final paragraph of moral exhortation (Mapple) or imprecation (Fleece). Nor should we forget that young Ishmael's crisp moral analogues (above) start with symbols and end as parables. It is especially interesting to note that some of the cetological chapters can be analyzed in terms of sermon structure. In "The Line," for instance, the narrator takes hemp for his text, makes a full-scale explication of its history and uses, gives admonitions on its subtleties and dangers, and concludes with a full-scale application of the doctrine that "All men live enveloped in whale-lines." In "The Blanket" the text is whale blubber; and preacher Ishmael comes inevitably to the doctrine of internal temperatures, raising it to a high exhortation (Mapple) and then cutting it down with three lines of wry counterstatement (Fleece). Nor is it hard to identify text, inferences, uses, doctrine, and admonition in the brief "sermon" the narrator preaches over the peeled white body of a whale in "The Funeral." The technique lies midway between the Protestant sermon of the nineteenth century and the tradition of the digressive-antiquarian essay.

Coming to the problem of the mutual relation of the chapters in *Moby-Dick*, we can observe several tendencies, of which *chapter sequences* is one. The simplest sequence is likely to be one of narrative progression, as in "The Chapel," "The Pulpit," and "The

Sermon," or in the powerful concluding sequence on "The Chase":
"First Day," "Second Day", "Third Day." Or we get chapter sequences of theme, as in the three chapters on whale paintings. Or
again sequences of structural similarity: the five chapters beginning
with "The Quarter-Deck" all use dramatic techniques, as do the four
beginning with "The Candles." More typical than strict sequences,
however, are the *chapter clusters* in which two or three (or five or
six) chapters are linked by themes or root images, other chapters
intervening. For example, chapters xlii, li, lii, and lix make a loose
cluster that begins with "The Whiteness of the Whale" and carries
through the white apparitions in "The Spirit-Spout," "The Albatross," and "Squid." Similarly, later in the narrative, fire imagery
becomes dominant, breaking out in young Ishmael's fire-dream
("The Try-Works") and running intermittently until the holocaust
of Ahab's defiance ("The Candles"). In addition to sequences and
clusters there are also widely separated *balancing chapters*, either
of opposites ("Loomings" and the "Epilogue") or of similars ("The
Quarter-Deck" and "The Candles"); here the problem is infinitely
complex, for the balancing units shift according to the standard of
comparison: theme, event, root image, structure, and so forth. Two
points can be made in tentative summary of this complex aspect of
structure: there are definable relations between any given chapter
and some other chapter or chapters; and these relations tend to be
multiple and shifting. Like the symbols, the chapters are "in
process."

Looking beyond chapter units and their interrelations we find the
most obvious larger structural effect in the narrative line of the
book, such as it is, which records the preparations for going on
board, leaving port, encountering adventures, and meeting some
final consequence. Along this simple linear form of The Voyage
occur two sets of events: the whale killings and the ship meetings.
The question is whether either of these event groups performs more
for the structure than the simple functions of marking the passage
of time and adding "interest." Of the whale pursuits and killings
some ten or more are sufficiently rendered to become events. They
begin when the narrative is already two-fifths told and end with the
final lowerings for Moby Dick during which the killers are themselves killed. The first lowering and the three-day chase are thus
events which enclose all the whaling action of the novel as well as
what Howard Vincent has aptly called "the cetological center," and
the main point I wish to make about the pursuits is that in each
case a killing provokes either a chapter sequence or a chapter
cluster of cetological lore growing out of the circumstances of the

particular killing. The killings in themselves, except for the first and last, are not so much narrative events as structural occasions for ordering the whaling essays and sermons. Their minimized role is proof enough, if any were needed, that Ishmael's tale is not primarily a series of whaling adventures.

Much more significant structurally than the killings is the important series of ship meetings also occurring along the time line of the voyage. The nine gams of the *Pequod* are important in several ways, of which three might concern us here. First of all, even a glance at the numbers of the chapters in which the gams occur shows a clear pattern: the first two are close together; the central group are well spaced (separated by an average of twelve chapters, with not very wide divergences); the last two are close together. The spatial pattern looks like this:

1 2   3   4   5   6   7   8 9

This somewhat mechanical pattern is a stiffening element in the structure of the book, a kind of counterforce, structurally, to the organic relationship of parts we have been observing. The gams are bones to the book's flesh. Secondly, their sequence is meaningful in terms of the Ahab theme. The line of Ahab's response from ship to ship is a psychograph of his monomania showing the rising curve of his passion and diagraming his moral hostility. The points on the graph mark off the furiously increasing distance between Ahab and the world of men. And thirdly, their individual meanings are a part of the Ishmael theme. Each ship is a scroll which the narrator unrolls and reads, like a prophet called to a king's court. They provide what Auden calls "types of the relation of human individuals and societies in the tragic mystery of existence," though his superbly incisive reading of each type is perhaps too narrowly theological and does scant justice to either the tone of the episodes (are not the *Jungfrau* and *Rosebud* accounts hilariously comic and ironic?) or their rich amplitude of meanings. The ships the *Pequod* passes may be taken as a group of metaphysical parables, a series of biblical analogues, a masque of the situations confronting man, a pageant of the humors within men, a parade of the nations, and so forth, *as well as* concrete and symbolic ways of thinking about the White Whale. Any single systematic treatment of all of the ships does violence to some of them. The gams are symbolic, not allegorical.

It is time in fact to admit that our explorations of structure suggest elaborate interrelations of the parts but do not lead to an overreaching formal pattern. For the reader predisposed to feel that

"form" means "classical form," with a controlling geometric structure, *Moby-Dick* is and will remain an aesthetically unsatisfying
experience. One needs only to compare it with *The Scarlet Letter*,
published a year and a half earlier, to see how nonclassical it is. If
this is the sort of standard by which one tries to judge *Moby-Dick*,
he will end by dismissing it as one of the more notable miscarriages
in the history of literary lying-in. But surely there is no one right
form the novel must take — not the one used by Hawthorne, not
even the form, one might wryly add, perfected by James. For Hawthorne the structural frame of reference was neoclassical; for Melville it was romantic.

To go from *The Scarlet Letter* to *Moby-Dick* is to move from the
Newtonian world-as-machine to the Darwinian world-as-organism.
In the older cosmology the key concepts had been law, balance,
harmony, reason; in the newer, they became origin, process, development, growth. Concurrently biological images arose to take the
place of the older mechanical analogies: growing plants and life
forms now symbolized cosmic ultimates better than a watch or the
slow-turning rods and gears of an eighteenth-century orrery. It is
enough for our purposes to note that the man who gave scientific
validity to the organic world view concluded the key chapter of his
great book, *The Origin of Species*, with an extended image of "the
great Tree of Life . . . with its ever branching and beautiful ramifi-
cations." It was a crucial simile that exploited not the tree but the
tree's growth.

Of course the poets had been there first. Coleridge had long since
made his famous definition of organic form in literature. The roots
of his theory had traveled under the sea to the continent of Emerson, Thoreau, and Whitman (as Matthiessen brilliantly showed in
American Renaissance), where they burst into native forms in the
minds of a few men haunted simultaneously by the implications of
the American wilderness, by the quest for spiritual reality, and by
the search for new literary forms. *Moby-Dick* is like Emerson's
Essays and *Poems*, like *Walden*, like *Leaves of Grass*, in its structural principles. In the literature of the nineteenth century it is the
single most ambitious projection of the concept of organic form.

Recharting our explorations we can see now where we have been.
The matter of *Moby-Dick* is the organic land-sea world where life
forms move mysteriously among the elements. The dynamic of the
book is the organic mind-world of Ishmael whose sensibility rhyth-
mically agitates the flux of experience. The controlling structure of
the book is an organic complex of rhetoric, symbols, and interfused

units. There is no over-reaching formal pattern of literary art on which *Moby-Dick* is a variation. To compare it with the structure of the Elizabethan play, or the classical epic, or the modern novel is to set up useful analogies rather than congruous models. It is a free form that fuses as best it can innumerable devices from many literary traditions, including contemporary modes of native expression. In the last analysis, if one must have a prototype, here is an intensively heightened rendition of the logs, journals, and histories of the Anglo-American whaling tradition.

Organic form is not a particular form but a structural principle. In *Moby-Dick* this principle would seem to be a peculiar quality of making and unmaking itself as it goes. The method of the book is unceasingly genetic, conveying the effect of a restless series of morphic-amorphic movements. Ishmael's narrative is always in process and in all but the most literal sense remains unfinished. For the good reader the experience of *Moby-Dick* is a participation in the act of creation. Find a key word or metaphor, start to pick it as you would a wild flower, and you will find yourself ripping up the whole forest floor. Rhetoric grows into symbolism and symbolism into structure; then all falls away and begins over again.

Ishmael's way of explaining himself in the long run is not either "dim" or "random." He was committed to the organic method with all its possibilities and risks. As he says at the beginning of one chapter: "There are some enterprises in which a careful disorderliness is the true method." And at the beginning of another chapter we have an explicit image whose full force as a comment on method needs to be recognized: "Out of the trunk, the branches grow; out of them, the twigs. So, in productive subjects, grow the chapters."

Leon Howard

The Creation of *Moby Dick*

By the time Melville returned home, on February 1, 1850, he seems to have laid aside his plan for the historical novel. At any rate, by May 1 he had seen *White Jacket* through the press and was able to write Richard Henry Dana, Jr., that he was "half way" in a book which he referred to as "the 'whaling voyage.'" And on June 27 he promised the completed volume to his English publisher "in the latter part of the coming autumn" and described it specifically but with some exaggeration as "a romance of adventure, founded upon certain wild legends in the Southern Sperm Whale Fisheries and illustrated by the author's own personal experience, of two years and more, as a harpooneer." In the middle of July he was ready for a vacation and left for Pittsfield, Massachusetts, where Evert Duyckinck visited him in early August and wrote that "Melville has a new book mostly done—a romantic, fanciful and literal and most enjoyable presentment of the Whale Fishery—something quite new."

Leon Howard, *Herman Melville*, University of Minnesota Pamphlets on American Writers, No. 13, University of Minnesota Press, Minneapolis, 18-25. © Copyright 1961, University of Minnesota.

These early references to the book which was to become *Moby Dick* are of unusual interest because they introduce the most teasing question which arises in any effort to follow the development of Melville's creative imagination: How did it happen that he was to spend a year of agonized composition upon a "mostly done" manuscript and transform it from a romance with autobiographical overtones into the powerfully dramatic novel it became? He seems to have had no intention, when he went on his vacation, of doing more than filling out his narrative with realistic details gathered from books of reference he had collected for that purpose. But once again the emotions of immediate experience were to project themselves into his fiction, transform it, and give it—this time—not only the vitality of his own life but the tensions of the century in which he lived.

The trigger action for his explosion into greatness was that of a single day, August 5, 1850, during his vacation when one of his neighbors arranged an expedition and dinner party for all the literary celebrities of the region—the New Englanders who summered in the Berkshires and Melville and the New York guests he had invited up for a visit. The expedition was to the top of Monument Mountain where Melville, Nathaniel Hawthorne, and Oliver Wendell Holmes were made gay by the elevation and champagne and brought back to sobriety by the New York critic Cornelius Mathews, who insisted upon making the occasion literary by reading William Cullen Bryant's solemn poem about the Indian lovers who had leaped to their death from the projecting ledge on which Melville had been performing sailor's antics. Holmes's satiric impulses were aroused, and the result was a literary quarrel which continued throughout the "well moistened" dinner party later. It focused upon the theory of the influence of climate upon genius and the question whether America would produce a literature as elevated as its mountains and as spacious as its plains. The New Englanders (as Holmes's Phi Beta Kappa poem *Astraea* of a few days later was to show) were skeptical of the New Yorkers' enthusiasm.

Melville's part in the argument seems to have been more mischievous than serious, but he was impressed by it and even more impressed by his first meeting with Hawthorne. His aunt had given him a copy of *Mosses from an Old Manse* at the beginning of his vacation, but he had not yet read it. Now, having met the author, he read it with the extraordinary enthusiasm he expressed in the belated review he wrote for the *Literary World* before his New York friends went home. Hawthorne proved the greatness of American literature, he contended, under the anonymous signature of "A Virginian spending July in Vermont"; but it was a greatness of heart and mind, observable in Hawthorne's willingness to present the "blackness" of truth — the same dark "background against which Shakespeare plays his grandest conceits" and which "appeals to that Calvinistic sense of Innate Depravity and Original Sin, from whose visitations, in some shape or other, no deeply thinking mind is always and wholly free." In Hawthorne and his *Mosses* Melville found an attitude of mind which courageously reflected all his doubts concerning the Transcendental idealism and optimism that had interested him during his recent voyage and had affected his reading since.

The impression made by Hawthorne was so great that Melville cultivated his acquaintance assiduously during the following months and eventually dedicated *Moby Dick* to him. Yet he did not become a wholehearted convert to his new friend's "black" skepticism. He was himself a man of greater vitality, more of a man of action, than Hawthorne; and although the two shared an interest in the Gothic Romance, Hawthorne's interest was in the Gothic atmosphere whereas Melville's was in the Romantic hero — the Byronic wandering outlaw of his own dark mind. Furthermore, Melville had borrowed *Sartor Resartus* at the time he finished collecting his whaling library for the revision of his book, and he found in Carlyle's Transcendentalized version of the Romantic hero a character who was as "deep-diving" as Emerson but who had proved himself susceptible to Hawthorne's pessimism and capable of defying it. In one of his stories in the *Mosses*, "Earth's Holocaust," Hawthorne had set forth allegorically his belief that evil could not be destroyed because it was constantly being recreated by "the all-engendering heart of man." Melville was inclined to agree. But the best "strong positive illustration" Melville found of the "blackness in Hawthorne" was in the story of "Young Goodman Brown" and his allegorical but unanswered cry for "Faith." In Carlyle's book Melville found a hero who could live in such a spiritual state of "starless, Tartarean black" that he could hear the Devil say "thou art fatherless, outcast, and the Universe is mine" but who still had the courage and the energy to say "*I* am not thine, but Free, and forever hate thee!" Whether he was as sensible as Young Goodman Brown (who went into a lethargy when he was convinced, either by a dream or by a real experience, that the world was the Devil's) might be questionable. But he was more heroic and, to Melville's mind, more admirable.

Melville's literary interests, in short, reveal the tensions that existed in his mind at the time he began what otherwise might have been the routine job of revising his manuscript. They were vital tensions, not only in terms of his own sensitivity but in their profound effect upon Western civilization during the nineteenth century—tensions set up by the conflict between the will to believe and the need to be shown, between Transcendentalism and empiricism in philosophy, between religion and science, between faith and skepticism. These were not tensions to be resolved, as so many of Melville's contemporaries tried to resolve them, for no satisfactory resolution has yet proved possible. Melville, at his deepest and most complex creative level, made no attempt to resolve the conflict. Instead, he dramatized it. And it may be that the ambiguity and ambivalence inherent in the dramatic Shakespearean qualities of *Moby Dick* are responsible for the fact that it has a greater appeal to the puzzled and questioning twentieth century than do the writings of Melville's contemporaries who were more explicitly concerned with the same tensions.

In any event, Shakespeare was an important element in the literary and intellectual ferment which went into the making of *Moby Dick*. Melville had become excited about him at the time he discovered Transcendentalism, in February 1849, when he wrote Evert Duyckinck that "if another Messiah ever comes twill be in Shakespeare's person." And he kept looking, in his review of the *Mosses*, if not for another Messiah at least for another Shakespeare — perhaps "this day being born on the banks of the Ohio." Hawthorne had "approached" him, for a nineteenth-century Shakespeare would not be an Elizabethan dramatist but a part of his "times" with "correspondent coloring." There is no doubt but that Melville was excited by the company and the literary debate of August 5, 1850, and it may have been that this excitement was intensified by a feeling of challenge. Within a few days he was to denounce the "absolute and unconditional adoration of Shakespeare" and his "unapproachability" as one of "our Anglo-Saxon superstitions." Might not he himself be another man "to carry republican progressiveness into Literature as well as into Life" by writing a novel that had the quality of Shakespearean tragedy?

However this might be, his novel began to change from a story of the whale fishery to a story of "the Whale." Captain Ahab (named for a man who had "done evil in the sight of the Lord") remained the protagonist in his narrative, but his antagonist was neither the worthy mate Starbuck nor any member of his exotic crew. It was the great white whale with a humped back and hieroglyphics on his brow, known throughout the fishery as Moby Dick and notorious for the viciousness with which he had turned upon the men who had hunted and attempted to destroy him. Ahab himself had been his victim on a previous voyage when the whale had sheared off his leg and started a train of cause and effect that resulted in his further mutilation by its splintered substitute. And Ahab, a queer "grand, ungodly, god-like man," had embarked on a voyage of revenge which would follow the paths of the migrating leviathan throughout the vast Pacific until he and the whole ship's crew were destroyed and the narrator alone was left to tell the tale. In order to make the voyage plausible Melville had to draw upon the whole body of available whaling lore in extraordinary detail. He also had to made his captain mad.

But the power of the book does not come from the realistic fantasy of the voyage or from the obsessed madness of the traditional Gothic or Romantic protagonist who is half hero and half villain. On the contrary, it comes from the fact that Ahab is one of the few characters in literature genuinely "formed for noble tragedies." Like Lear, he is a noble individual whose only flaw is a single mistake in judgment. And like Hamlet, at least as Coleridge interpreted him, his mistake is that of a disordered judgment — that of a man with a "craving after the indefinite" who "looks upon external things as hieroglyphics" and whose mind, with its "everlasting broodings," is "unseated from its healthy relation" and "constantly occupied with the world within, and abstracted from the world without — giving substance to shadows, and throwing a mist over all commonplace actualities." For to Ahab "all visible objects" were "but as pasteboard masks" from behind which "some unknown but still reasoning thing puts forth the mouldings of its features." To him the white whale was the emblem of "outrageous strength, with inscrutable malice sinewing it"; and it was "that inscrutable thing" which he hated, and he was determined to "wreak that hate upon him."

Whether Ahab's attitude should be interpreted in psychological or philosophical terms is an important question with respect to Melville's biography. The narrator, Ishmael, uses psychological terms in his accounts of the phases Ahab goes through while "deliriously transferring" his idea of evil to the whale as an object which would visibly personify it and make it practically assailable. Ahab himself, of course, sounds like Carlyle's hero asserting his individual freedom and defying the Devil's claim to the universe. The weight of the evidence, derived from the book and from letters written at the same time, appears to favor a rather close identification of the author's point of view with that of the narrator. Melville's conscious fable in *Moby Dick* seems to lead to the conclusion that a belief in the emblematic nature of the universe is a form of madness. His rational judgment apparently concurred with that of Hawthorne: the white whale was a natural beast, and the evil in him was a product of the "all-engendering heart" or mind of Ahab. But, for the moment, Melville's personal philosophy is not relevant to an interpretation of *Moby Dick* as a work of literature. "Dramatically regarded," as he himself put it, "all men tragically great are made so through a certain morbidness." The important point is that Ahab's "morbidness," whether a sane conviction or a mad obsession, was the tragic flaw in his character which directed his heroic behavior toward destruction.

Yet if one goes beyond superficial interpretation into an attempt to explain the strange power of *Moby Dick*, Melville's personal beliefs do become important and his chapter on "The Whiteness of the Whale" becomes particularly relevant. For here he collects evidence for the existence of a sort of knowledge which is more intuitive than the rational empiricism used by Ishmael to explain "crazy Ahab" in the immediately preceding chapter. The inference to be drawn is that Melville was not wholly convinced of the validity of the fable his rational mind constructed in order to provide himself with a plot of the sort he found and admired in Hawthorne. The conflict between Transcendentalism and empiricism was not something which he merely observed and then dramatized. It was something that he experienced and felt deeply within himself. Ahab, who sometimes doubted whether there was anything beyond the "wall" of the emblematic material universe, was only slightly more mad than the storyteller who condemned him but sometimes doubted whether the material world of experience provided the ultimate form of knowledge. Melville could easily imagine within himself the rage to believe, the madness, he attributed to his hero as a "tragic flaw."

Nathalia Wright

Mosses from an Old Manse and *Moby-Dick*
The Shock of Discovery

Moby-Dick presents the curious problem of an author's unquestionable masterpiece which, in terms of everything else he wrote, is an anomaly. In this novel Melville's unseen world is supernatural rather than metaphysical, revenge is a stronger motive than envy in demonic action, the blond image is superseded by the image of fire. Whence did these variations in pattern come? In part the answer seems to be: from Hawthorne's *Mosses from an Old Manse*, which Melville read in the summer of 1850, when he was midway in the composition of his whaling romance. In his review of the volume for *The Literary World* he acknowledged "the shock of recognition"[1] he received upon encountering the proposition, fundamental to his own thought, that intellect and feeling are mutually dependent and should be so treated in fiction. But the shock of discovering that this proposition might be expressed in totally different terms remained to be recorded in the characterization and imagery of *Moby-Dick*.

Modern Language Notes (June, 1952), pp. 387-392. By permission of The Johns Hopkins Press.
[1]Willard Thorp, ed., *Herman Melville. Representative Selections* (New York, American Book Co., c 1938), p. 339.

When Melville wrote *Mardi*, his first consciously artistic creation, he projected a metaphysical and moral allegory whose main outlines are recognizable in everything he wrote thereafter. In the prevailing terms of this allegory, the ideal man combines a cool head and a warm heart, whereas the two principal imperfect character types, the intellectual and the sensualist, develop only one of these members. The chief characteristic of the head is envious aggression, a concept which links it with the demon principle, whereas the heart by its passivity is associated with the deity principle. Symbolic of these two principles is the dark-light antithesis which is Melville's most persistent image.

But Ahab is not only the intellectual in revolt, like Lucifer; he is, alone among Melville's characters, the intellectual as black magician, like Faust.[2] He is committed to Fedallah, who is called "the Devil" and "Beelzebub"; he dominates the crew by a hypnotic gaze and breath; he performs a series of pseudo-scientific experiments which aim to circumvent nature; he is blasphemous; he evokes primarily the image of fire. He is also mutilated and vengeful.

The type is common in Hawthorne: the man of intellect endowed with scientific or artistic wizardry and, in the degree to which he is villainous, with a diabolical, hypnotic power, deformity, and vengeance. In the *Mosses*[3] it appears in nearly a third of the selections. Two of them contain allusions to the Faust theme. Two others exhibit more detailed parallels with Ahab's story. The *Pequod's* blacksmith, Perth, resembles Aylmer's servant Aminidab in "The Birthmark": hairy and sooty from working at his forge, less sensitive than his master—whose sleep is disturbed by dreams,[4] executing orders without understanding them, but unable to eradicate the scar which is a birthmark. The witches' communion and baptism in "Young Goodman Brown" have several points in common with Ahab's travesties of the same religious ceremonies and his fire worship. Brown arrives near midnight in the midst of a

---

[2] In Goethe's poem, however, which may have been among the books by him which Melville read in 1849-51, the characterization lacks the overdeveloped head-underdeveloped heart pattern.

[3] The last two characteristics of the type are not as clearly represented in this volume, however, as they are in the other books by Hawthorne which Melville read in 1850-51: *Twice Told Tales, The House of the Seven Gables,* and probably *The Scarlet Letter.*

[4] Melville scored this episode in his copy of the *Mosses,* which is now in the Harvard College Library. Another earthy blacksmith in Hawthorne's volume is Robert Danforth in "The Artist of the Beautiful." The relationship of Prospero and Caliban was probably in the minds of both authors.

tempest at an altar-like rock, surrounded by four pines whose tops
are flaming "like candles at an evening meeting," where new members are brought into "communion";[5] the trees suddenly blaze
higher as the Devil prepares to baptize the converts from a basin
containing blood or another red liquid. Ahab uses the harpoon
sockets as "chalices" in which to serve the grog "hot as Satan's
hoof"; he baptizes his whale barbs in the blood of the harpooners,
shouting "Ego non baptizo te in nomine patris, sed in nomine diaboli!"; in the chapter entitled "The Candles" he worships, in the
midst of the midnight typhoon and in the guise of "Old Thunder,"
the corposants burning at the tops of the masts — "three gigantic
wax tapers before an altar," which at his invocation leap thrice their
height.[6]

The fire imagery in *Moby-Dick* is more complex, however, than
that which commonly accompanies the black magic theme. Here
fire, which characteristically in Melville's head-heart configuration
is a minor symbol of the human heart, attracts the head and functions equally with whiteness as the deity principle. But it has affin-
ities with both the demonic and the divine; it is both mechanistic
and creative. Ahab transforms his Anarcharsis Clootz crew into a
body "brave as fearless fire (and as mechanical)"; his inanimate leg
is finished at the blacksmith's forge; gazing into the "artificial fire,"
in whose light the crew seem fiends, Ishmael almost capsizes the
Pequod. But the element sacred to the Persians and the Greeks is
also here: the purpose of the try-works is to transmute the whale
into oil, which purifies the ship and illumines the world; as a man-
maker, Ahab, who calls himself a Greek god, is as Promethean as he
considers Perth when he says, "I do deem it now a most meaning
thing, that that old Greek, Prometheus, who made men, they say,
should have been a blacksmith, and animated them with fire."[7]

Now a general fire imagery is diffused through all Hawthorne
wrote, dominates half the selections in the *Mosses*, and twice em-
bodies the author's theme and furnishes his title. "Fire Worship"
alone contains most of the specific fire images which occur in *Moby-
Dick*: the Promethean theft of the divine fire, volcanic eruptions,

---

[5] *Mosses from an Old Manse* (Boston, Houghton, c 1882), pp. 100, 97.
[6] *Moby-Dick* (London, Constable, 1922), I, 207, 206; II, 261, 279. The letter in
which Melville told Hawthorne the baptismal pronouncement was the secret
motto of the book suggests that it was familiar to Hawthorne, for Melville
broke off in an otherwise inexplicable manner, *"Ego non baptiso te in
nomine —* but make out the rest yourself." (Julian Hawthorne, *Nathaniel
Hawthorne and his Wife*. Boston, Osgood, 1885, I, 400.)
[7] *Moby-Dick*, II, 341 (see also 352), 181, 237.

lightning, Zoroastrian fire worship,[8] prairie fires, the forge's light, the burning pipe, the hearth, the infernal pit, the removal of one's shoes before treading supernaturally burning ground, fire as a mirror reflecting the thoughts of the fire-gazer.[9] This essay, moreover, is constructed by a technique more characteristic of Melville than of Hawthorne: the placing of a primary image or symbol at the center of a cluster of secondary images, as in the chapter on the whiteness of the whale.[10]

Furthermore, Hawthorne's fire imagery, which occurs most often in connection with his intellectual wizards, also possesses a double signification: it suggests a mechanistic principle in such pieces as "The Birthmark," "The Celestial Railroad," and "The Artist of the Beautiful," and a purifying, restorative principle in such as "Earth's Holocaust" (Melville referred to its "allegorical fire" in his review) and "A Virtuoso's Collection" — or, as they might be called, a false and a true creative principle. His allusions to the Promethean theme, too, allow for the same dualism: the true Prometheus is a giant capable of reaching heaven, recognized in "Earth's Holocaust" as being a rare achievement; yet the fire thus obtained may be abused, as it is when the Virtuoso introduces a salamander into it.[11]

Yet in the very act of discovering Hawthorne's pattern of intellectual diabolism Melville altered it in significant details. Unlike Hawthorne, he distinguished between two kinds of magic: black and white, or as his annotations in his set of Shakespeare expressed it, "Not the (black art) Goetic but Theurgic magic — seeks con-

---

[8] In "Rappaccini's Daughter" Hawthorne describes this essay as " 'Le Culte du Feu,' a folio volume of ponderous research into the religion and ritual of the old Persian Ghebers." (*Mosses from an Old Manse*, p. 108.)

[9] This image recurs in "Sketches from Memory," wherein Hawthorne records that he so forgot himself looking at a phosphorescent decayed tree on the banks of the Erie Canal that he allowed the boat to depart without him.

[10] The total structure of the *Mosses*, in fact, is comparable to *Moby-Dick's:* the alternation between Hawthorne's tales and sketches, like that between Melville's narrative and expository chapters, is technically an alternation between scene and panorama. But Melville's peculiar dependence upon exposition, from *Typee* on, made some such development as this inevitable.

[11] Many parallels exist also in the general imagery of the two books: the faces of Robert Burns in "P.'s Correspondence" and of Elijah in *Moby-Dick* are furrowed like the bed of a torrent; the narrator of "Buds and Bird Voices" says men must ever be susceptible to spring (Melville quoted from the passage in his review), and wintry Ahab puts forth green sprouts a few days after the *Pequod* sets sail; had the New Adam read through the Harvard Library he would have staggered under the burden of mankind's accumulated knowledge, like Ahab, who feels on the day before the chase that he is Adam carrying the weight of the intervening centuries.

verse with the Intelligence, Power, the Angel."[12] Hawthorne himself seemed to him a practitioner of this art, a "wizard" with a
"wild, witch-voice," whose "spell" had "witched" him in the *Mosses*,
who was able, in praising *Moby-Dick*, to embrace "the ugly Socrates
because you saw the flame in the mouth, and heard the rushing of
the demon, the familiar, — and recognized the sound; for you have
heard it in your own solitudes."[13] In Melville's novels, however, the
white or undiabolical approach to truth is not confined to the intellectual sphere, and is more often depicted in terms of the madness
than of the "right reason" which composed, as his Shakespeare annotations said, "the extremes of one": the seizures of Babbalanja
by his devil Azzageddi, the lunacy of Pip.

Unlike Hawthorne also, Melville persisted in regarding fire as primarily a symbol of the emotional and social rather than the intellectual life. In his review of the *Mosses* he quoted the two passages
from "The Intelligence Office" and "A Select Party" which most
nearly match Babbalanja's description of the ideal, warm-hearted,
cool-headed man, and repeatedly hailed the author as a man of
glowing heart. His comment on the character of Ethan Brand[14]
actually contradicts Hawthorne's imagistic meaning, for, posing
that men of true intellect have hearts extending to their hams, it
concluded, "And though you smoke them with the fire of tribula-
tion, yet, like veritable hams, the head only gives the richer and the
better flavor."[15]

With *Pierre* Melville returned to his own peculiar patterns of
characterization and imagery in which to restate the problem, pre-
occupying both him and Hawthorne, of the relationship between the
head and the heart, the intellect and the feeling, the demonic and

[12]Melville's Shakespeare is in the Harvard College Library. The two pages of
annotations which consist largely of notes for a projected tale of a compact
between the Devil and a human soul and contain a version of the "Ego non
baptizo" line have been transcribed by Jay Leyda in his introduction to *The
Complete Stories of Herman Melville* (New York, Random House, c 1949),
p. xi.

[13]Thorp, *op. cit.*, pp. 330, 394, 328, 333, 394.

[14]Brand's last words, "O Mother Earth . . . who art no more my Mother, and
into whose bosom this frame shall never be resolved! . . . Come, deadly element of Fire,—henceforth my familiar friend! Embrace me, as I do thee!" are
echoed in Ahab's invocation, "Oh! thou clear spirit of clear fire. . . . I will
kneel and kiss thee. . . . But thou art but my fiery father; my sweet mother, I
know not. . . . I leap with thee; I burn with thee; would fain be welded with
thee. . . ." (*The House of the Seven Gables and The Snow-Image and Other
Twice-Told Tales* (Boston, Houghton, c 1883), p. 496; *Moby-Dick*, II, 281-
283). Melville read Hawthorne's story in *The Dollar Magazine* for May 1851.

[15]Thorp, *op. cit.*, p. 392.

the divine. Five years later the shock of discovering Hawthorne's patterns was still strong enough for Melville to make Bannadonna in "The Bell-Tower" a scientific artist, working with fire. But Bannadonna's complete materialism is more terrible than any pact with evil spirits. If for no other reason, Melville must ultimately have found the Faustian configuration inadequate because of his deepening perception of this great peril of the machine age.

M. O. Percival

[Captain Ahab
and Moby Dick]

Who, it is now pertinent to ask, is this Captain Ahab, the hunter, and what is this Moby Dick, the hunted?

Ahab was born to greatness, even to tragic greatness, and this, the author says, always implies a certain morbidness of character. Symptoms of a tragic destiny appeared in early infancy. Something in his behavior, something not mentioned but easily imagined, revealed to his mother's anxious eye the fatal dower. The man, she foresaw, would be both kingly and blasphemous; he would be an Ahab. And so, to his fatal inheritance she added the fatal increment of a wicked name. The mother's intuition was confirmed by the old squaw Tistig at Gayhead, who said that the name would somehow prove prophetic. So dowered, so named, and subject to such a prophecy, how should he escape the part allotted to him in "the grand programme of Providence that was drawn up a long time ago"?

The mother's intuition was confirmed, again, by Ahab's character and conduct as a whaling captain. The "boiling blood" and

From *A Reading of Moby-Dick* (Chicago: The University of Chicago Press, 1950), pp. 14-23.

the "smoking brow" when a boat was lowered for a whale are not too disquieting; but there was something mysterious and ominous in his temperament, something which Ishmael, lacking the terminology of depth psychology, tries to suggest by the metaphor of deep and dark recesses in the earth. The roots of his nature strike deep down into these lower levels of consciousness. In everything that Ahab does, the unconscious drive is operating upon the conscious purpose; it is this that gives power and plausibility to his character. From this deep source comes his physical and mental energy, both demonic. Little wonder that he perseveres in a course which he knows to be both desperate and mad, that he prefers martyrdom to repentance, that he is proud of the demon that possesses and destroys him.

The fate that the mother dimly apprehended is forecast also in certain outbursts of fury in Ahab's life, prior to this, the final chapter. Elijah, who knows his Ahab, hints darkly at them. Have you not heard, he inquires, "about that thing that happened to him off Cape Horn, long ago, when he lay like dead for three days and nights; nothing about that deadly skrimmage with the Spaniard afore the altar in Santa?—heard nothing about that, eh? Nothing about the silver calabash he spat into?" From these strange fits of passion he recovered, but on the last voyage, in the waters off Japan, he suffered an injury which evoked his fate. A certain white whale, of almost legendary fame for malevolence and ferocity, "dismasted" him:

> His three boats stove around him, and oars and men both whirling in the eddies; one captain, seizing the line-knife from his broken prow, had dashed at the whale, as an Arkansas duellist at his foe, blindly seeking with a six inch blade to reach the fathom-deep life of the whale. That captain was Ahab. And then it was, that suddenly sweeping his sickle-shaped lower jaw beneath him, Moby Dick had reaped away Ahab's leg, as a mower a blade of grass in the field.

The dismemberment drove him frantic. For days and weeks and months on the voyage home, "Ahab and anguish lay stretched together in one hammock." Anguish reached such a pitch that Ahab had to be confined in a strait jacket, in which, mad himself, he "swung to the mad rockings of the gales." Finally, the madness subsided into quiet desperation, into a settled, mad resolve to be avenged.

These are the facts. The psychological processes behind them, if discoverable, would make an illuminating page in the book of human nature. Now it so happened that a contemporary of Ahab's, over in Denmark, underwent a variety and extremity of suffering almost, as he thought, unparalleled and then, with an insight almost unparalleled, he analyzed certain problems of suffering, including Ahab's. I refer, of course, to Soren Kierkegaard, some of whose insights I shall make use of.

The problem is despair. The blow falls, in one or another of its countless ways; the suffering seems beyond all measure and desert; the sufferer feels himself singled out—elected, as it were, to be the sport and jest of some malevolent deity. The initial reaction is despair. For a person cut off in this way from the universal pattern and marked out as a sacrifice, there are, says Kierkegaard, two eventualities: he will become demonic or essentially religious.

For a healthy nature there would seem to be release just short of an experience essentially religious. Infinite resignation, as Kierkegaard calls it, even without Christian faith, will bring peace. In the Stoic resignation there was peace, but a hard peace, dictated by pride. There is the example of Diogenes, of whom Epictetus says: "Hadst thou seized upon his possessions, he would rather have let them go than have followed thee for them—aye, had it been even a limb." But Ahab was too passionate and self-willed to make the gesture of infinite resignation. From a child he had been rebellious. The Stoic could submit himself to Providence. He could knit his mutilated spirit into the spirit of the universe. But not Ahab. "Who's over me?" he demands of Starbuck, in response to an expostulation. Stubb, who knew him well, reports that he never saw him kneel.

There remains the Christian way of resignation, the only way, according to Kierkegaard, whereby a morbid nature, passionate and self-willed, can encounter despair and conquer it. If the sufferer can say: "Before thee, O God, I am nothing, do with me as thou wilt," he will be able to bear the burden. He can lose the self, and then, by the well-known Christian paradox, regain it. But of Christian feeling there is no trace in Ahab. All the ways of resignation are therefore closed.

The alternative, in Kierkegaard's analysis, is defiance. Since the sufferer cannot lose himself, his one recourse is to affirm himself. The despair is not thereby cured. There is despair in the very effort to combat despair. As the consciousness of self increases, the despair increases, while the increasing despair increases the consciousness of self. The cycle thus set in motion has an inevitable outcome: the sufferer becomes demonic.

An important stage in Ahab's progress from the blind rage of complete despair to a rage partially subdued and organized under mad direction is reached in an incident which occurred before the "Pequod" sailed, although it is not described until long afterward. It is postponed, I suppose, in order that the element of allegory might readily be perceived. Ahab had returned home, the "Pequod" was getting ready, when one night he fell and was discovered lying upon the ground, helpless and insensible. "His ivory limb [had] been so violently displaced, that it had stake-wise smitten, and all but pierced his groin; nor was it without extreme difficulty that the agonizing wound was entirely cured." In this incident we find that Moby Dick — present in the ivory stake — had bitten into the very center of his being, leaving a wound that was to prove incurable. But Kierkegaard would see something more — a push toward the demonic. The incident included a twofold psychic trauma — the initial humiliation in his own eyes and the subsequent humiliation arising from compassion on the part of others. To be lifted out of the universal pattern, to be an object of humiliation to one's self and an object of compassion to others—this torture, more than any other, says Kierkegaard, tempts man to rebel against God. It can be borne only by resignation. But if it is combined with a passionate self-will, "then it will end with the sufferer losing his reason." As an instance of self-will turning the sufferer demonic, Kierkegaard cites Richard III. Of despair referred to God and turning into triumph, he is his own example. In the case of Ahab, it was this fall, hushed up by the few friends who knew about it, that sent him into a lama-like seclusion in his cabin—a seclusion from which he did not emerge until, turned demonic, he took his place upon the quarter-deck, prepared and determined to league his crew into a solemn oath to seek revenge upon Moby Dick.

And now, what of Moby Dick, the hunted?

He is a more mysterious being than Ahab, the hunter. On the level of plain fact he is simply a legendary white whale, the object of an exciting chase. On the level of allegory he is the presence of evil in the world, and his whiteness is both essential and mysterious. It was on the voyage home that Moby Dick was transformed from the particular to the universal, from fact to symbol:

> All that most maddens and torments; all that stirs up the lees of things; all truth with malice in it; all that cracks the sinews and cakes the brain; all the subtle demonisms of life and thought; all evil, to crazy Ahab, were visibly personified, and made practically

assailable in Moby Dick. He piled upon the whale's white hump the sum of all the general rage and hate felt by his whole race from Adam down; and then, as if his chest had been a mortar, he burst his hot heart's shell upon it.

It is as if, in the turmoil of Ahab's mind, an ancient superstition had risen into consciousness — the superstition of the scapegoat. Upon the head of an innocent animal were placed symbolically the sins of the whole community, and the animal was then sanctified and slain. But the object of Ahab's pursuit is the whole world's scapegoat, laden in his imagination with the whole world's evil. There is a difference, however, between the primitive scapegoat and Moby Dick. For Moby Dick is not an innocent animal bearing the world's evil; he is, in Ahab's sight, the evil without the innocence, and without the sanctification. The slaying of him, therefore, cannot be redemptive. This Ahab does not clearly see. He believes, or half-believes, that vengeance may have a redemptive quality. Mistaken as he is, however, Moby Dick has been transformed, in his imagination, from fact to symbol, though without losing, for the crew, his identity as a fact. The story moves on both levels to the end. The "unearthy conceit that Moby Dick was ubiquitous; that he had actually been encountered in opposite latitudes at one and the same instant of time," suggests the ubiquity of evil; but, at the same time, there is an effort, surely strained, to make the conceit plausible in fact. The reports of some whalers that Moby Dick was not only ubiquitous but immortal, that, "though groves of spears should be planted in his flanks, he would still swim away unharmed" — this report, on the allegorical level, is too obvious to state. More subtle is the report that Moby Dick's ferocity often seems deliberate, conscious, and intelligent. (How often we feel like saying that when the blow falls!) The terror he inspires is such that some think him supernatural or nearly so, and the terror seems to lie mainly in his color. His wrinkled brow is snow-white, and he carries a vast white hump. This "grand hooded phantom, like a snow hill in the air," is the mysterious monster that Ishmael went to sea to behold and ponder over. This is the devil incarnate that Ahab has willed to wrestle with and slay.

The supreme element in the terror Moby Dick inspires — his dazzling whiteness — is a mystery so baffling that Ishmael, who discourses on it, takes up the theme with a sense of inevitable failure. He says:

Aside from those more obvious considerations touching Moby Dick, which could not but occasionally awaken in any man's soul some alarm, there was another thought, or rather vague, nameless horror concerning him, which at times by its intensity completely overpowered all the rest; and yet so mystical and well nigh ineffable was it, that I almost despair of putting it in a comprehensible form. It was the whiteness of the whale that above all things appalled me. But how can I hope to explain myself here; and yet, in some dim, random way, explain myself I must, else all these chapters might be naught.

I, too, must take up the burden, for we have Ishmael's plain word for it that the central meaning of the book lies in this chapter.

The core of the chapter is simply this: that white is capable of two contrary effects. On the one hand, it is the emblem of innocence, honor, and purity; of the mystery of justice and the beauty of holiness; of whatever, in short, is sweet and honorable and sublime. On the other hand, it expresses the deepest terror that man knows; it is a bleak and desolate color; it is instinctively associated with the world's malevolence. There is a gigantic ghastliness in the wind-blown snows of the prairies, in the white scenery of the Antarctic, in the snow-capped mountains. It is a strange paradox that the same color should be "at once the most meaning symbol of spiritual things, nay, the very veil of the Christian's Deity; and yet should be as it is, the intensifying agent in things the most appalling to mankind." Divested of its investiture in white, it is the paradox of good and evil being ultimately one.

But, when the white inheres in the white whale, and particularly in its white hump, rising up like a snow hill in the air, the color and its paradox become alive, with a life keyed into the mystery and majesty of the great Leviathan. Here now, in a superlative degree, is an image of the kind beloved by contemporary poets, one expressing a whole complex of thought and emotion and fusing, in this instance, a variety of opposites, such as beauty and desolation, holiness and demonism, what is of good report and what of bad—more simply, good and evil. For some readers the symbol would carry a still deeper significance. For them the mysterious fusion of those contraries in Moby Dick would be but a reflection, in the somewhat deceptive world of sense, of the union of moral contraries, and, indeed, of all contraries, in the world of ultimate reality. The Hindus, for example, believe that the contraries are united in Brahma and in Krishna, his avatar. The following lines refer to Krishna:

> I heard the passion breathed amid the honeysuckle
>   scented glade,
> And saw the King pass lightly from the beauty that
>   he had betrayed.

I saw him pass from love to love; and yet the pure
  allowed his claim
To be the purest of the pure, thrice holy, stainless,
  without blame.

That, as the reader has probably recognized, is "A. E.," and here
he is in prose:

> The sphere of the argumentative intellect is the world where all
> things exist by way of balance of opposites, where for every black
> there is a white, and for every *pro* a *con*; and, if we lived only by
> the intellect, there could be no progress, for argument could be met
> by equal argument. "An eye for an eye, and a tooth for a tooth" is
> the justice of the intellect, and that warfare may go on for ever. We
> can only escape from an eternity of opposites by rising above them
> like that spirit which fixed the balance in the heavens and made
> equal centrifugal and centripetal. It was that spirit which would
> fain have admitted man to its own sphere, showing how to escape
> from the dominion of the opposites by rising above them. It coun-
> selled forgiveness until seventy times seven — a hard saying, no
> doubt, to those who have just cause for offence. But it is the only
> way by which we can be melted and made one in the higher
> spheres. . . .

Similarly, Blake asked, in a famous poem, whether it was possible
to believe that he who made the lamb also made the tiger. Not only
possible but necessary. And the first article of Blake's message to
the world is this: Inquire not into the mystery of good and evil. To
separate them apart and brood over them — to bring them under
the scrutiny of a doubting head and a selfish heart is to open the
gates of hell. By this action Adam fell; by this action the children
of Adam have been falling to this day.

R. W. B. Lewis

[*Moby-Dick* and Homer]

For the author of *Moby-Dick*, the central strain in the European tradition was tragic. The tragic sensibility defined in the long quotation from the "Try-Works" is attributed to books as well as to men: "That mortal man who hath more of joy than sorrow in him, that mortal man cannot be true — not true or undeveloped. With books the same." There, plainly enough, is an antihopeful judgment, and almost the reverse of it can be read on many pages of Emerson and Thoreau. But there is a point beyond that, which has to do with the creative process itself; and we should recall the actual experience out of which Ishmael's meditation rises, for the enterprise of trying-out was an explicit trope for Melville of the act of creativity. He wrote Dana, while at work on *Moby-Dick*, that the novel would be "a strange sort of book . . . blubber is blubber you know; though you might get oil out of it, the poetry runs as hard as sap from a frozen maple-tree." And since trying-out was associated in the story with so hellish a scene and nightmarish an experience, it

From *The American Adam* (Chicago: The University of Chicago Press, 1955), pp. 139-145.

is hard to resist the inference that creativity for Melville was closely, dangerously, associated with the monstrous vision of evil. You have to go through hell, he suggests, either to get the oil or to write the book.

Melville, that is to say, belongs to the company of gifted romantics from Blake and Baudelaire to Thomas Mann, who have supposed that art is somehow the flower of evil and that the power through which the shaping imagination is raised to greatness may also be a power which destroys the artist; for it is the strength derived from the knowledge of evil — not the detached study, but perhaps a very descent into the abyss. At some stage or other, Melville felt, art had to keep an appointment with wickedness. He believed with Hawthorne that, in order to achieve moral maturity, the individual had to engage evil and suffer the consequences; and he added the conviction that, in order to compose a mature work of literature, the artist had to enter without flinching into the "spheres of fright." For Melville, the two experiences happened not to be separable.

But how, having looked into the fire, was the artist to articulate his vision of evil in language? Still another clue is provided by the "Try-Works." It can scarcely be a coincidence that, after the slices of blubber (the source of oil) have been pointedly referred to as "Bible leaves," the insight gained from the spectacle is conveyed by Ishmael in a cluster of biblical references. The "Bible leaves" are passed through the furnaces, and oil is the result; similarly, Melville hints, the formed and incrusted language of the past must be "tried-out" in the transforming heat of the imagination, and the result is the shaped perception which can light up the work of art.

The transforming process was crucial, for Melville never simply echoed the words of the great books of the past; he subjected them to tremendous pressure and forced them to yield remarkable new revelations. His characterizing "relation to tradition" was extremely ambiguous: it was no more the willing enslavement exemplified by the nostalgic than it was the blithe patriotic indifference manifested by the hopeful. I take his reading and his treatment of the *Odyssey* of Homer as a major illustration of Melville's "trying-out" of a traditional poem.

Melville's Homer, like Keats's, was the Homer of George Chapman. He acquired the Chapman translations in 1858 and preferred them at once to the translations by Pope, which he probably read (and read carefully) as early as 1848.[1] What impresses us at once as we follow his check-marks, underlinings, and marginal comments through the poems is this: that Melville was a creative reader; he was the poet as reader who became the reader as poet. His markings, rarely casual or isolated, fall usually upon essential threads and force the poems to yield the figure within them. But it is Melville's figure, and not always the figure we are accustomed to discover ourselves.

His responsive reader's effect upon the *Iliad* is, to be sure, less conspicuous than its effect upon the *Odyessy*. The *Iliad*, under Melville's inspection, emerges as the somber portrait of a world at war, or sorrowing men caught up in vast forces and moving without hope to the violent death which awaits them, under the rule of implacable divinities. This is perhaps the *Iliad* we too are disposed to see; though it was not the *Iliad* of Melville's contemporary, Emerson, whose hopeful reading showed him only the "firm and cheerful temper" of a Homer who lay in the sunshine. But Melville read the *Odyssey* on a more symbolic level; his markings lead it to take the form of a tragic *Bildungsroman*, with the relation between the characters and the sequence of events standing for growth of insight into the heart of reality. There is evidence of Melville's immense enjoyment of the adventures themselves; but he was primarily interested in meaning.

The meaning Melville found borrows force from the unusual emphasis his markings laid upon the griefs and hardships of Odysseus and the generalizations about the evil lot of mankind, to the point where a rich and spacious poem looks surprisingly gloomier than we remembered it. Melville seized upon the recurring descriptions of Odysseus and his dwindling crew sailing on, stricken at heart after some frightful encounter; and he made much of the hero's artful lament to Nausicäa that he was the victim of "a cruel habit of calamity" (vi, 257). He marked the disclaimer of Telemachus:

---

[1]Cf. Merton M. Sealts, Jr., "Melville's Reading: A Check-List of Books Owned and Borrowed," *Harvard Library Bulletin*, Vol. III, No. 2 (spring, 1949), pp. 268 ff. I quote from a letter Mr. Sealts kindly wrote to me, February 21, 1949: "On 19 March 1848 HM was charged with '1 Classical Library, 37 v. 12.23.' ... Pope's Homer constitutes three of the volumes." Melville purchased the complete works of Pope at some time after 1856. Mr. Sealts concludes: "He may have known [Pope's Homer] before *Moby-Dick* or even as early as his days at the Albany Academy, though that last is pure speculation. He *almost* bought a Chapman's Homer in London" in 1849.

                          Not by any means
      If Hope should prompt me or *blind confidence*
      (*The God of fools*) or ever deity
      Should will it, for 'tis past my destiny.
                                    [iii. 309—Melville's italics.]

And the reaction of Telemachus to the dishonor shown his father:

              Never more let any sceptre-bearing man
              Benevolent, or mild, or human be,
              Nor in his mind form acts of piety,
              But ever feed on blood [ii. 348].

   The gods are no more benevolent than they had been in Melville's
Iliad. There they had comprised a remote and hostile race, indifferent to man and interfering in his affairs only to blast his tenuous
hopes; here Melville obtrudes Nestor's observation that "I know
God studied misery to hurl against us" (iii). By focusing attention
on these lines and many more like them, Melville forced the *Odyssey*
to move perceptibly, to shift and re-form; he exposed within it a
vision of terror and evil which casts a deep shadow over the beauty
and steady assurance the poem could otherwise be seen to reflect.
   That vision is the frame for the educational process Melville
traces for us. The process begins with the departure of Telemachus
for sandy Pylos and the admonitions of his nurse and his mother,
both of which are strongly checked:

                       It fits not you so young
              To suffer so much by the aged seas
              And err in such a wayless wilderness [ii. 545].

              Why left my son his mother? Why refused
              His wit the solid shore to try the seas
              And put in ships the trust of his distress
              That are at sea to man unbridled horse,
              And run past rule? [iv. 492.]

The echoes of Redburn and of Melville's personal life and relation
to his mother are clear. Going to sea, both in deed and in symbol,
was always Melville's way of fronting what Thoreau called "the
essential facts of life"; and what must be stressed is that the venture was so much the more harrowing for Melville because malice
and evil were central among the facts to be fronted. As he read on

in the *Odyssey*, Melville ran a line alongside Proteus' warning to Menelaus, indicative of the dangerous nature of the venture:

> Cease
> To ask so far. It fits not to be
> So cunning in thine own calamity.
> Nor seek to learn what learned thou shouldst forget.
> Men's knowledges have proper limits set.
> And should not prease into the mind of God [iv. 657].

Melville's conviction about the peril did not prevent his own heroes from making the plunge nevertheless and "preasing" with all their might into the mind of God: into whatever it was which lay behind the appearances of things; and so they all "suffered so much by the aged seas." It is with the suffering and the lies and the silence of the much-buffeted Odysseus that Melville's pencilings of the *Odyssey* come to an end.

Having noticed Homer's observation (vi. 198) that "the hard pass [Odysseus] had at sea stuck by him," and, having digested the obvious fabrications with which Odysseus regaled the court of Antinöus, Melville greeted the wanderer's decision, upon arriving at last in Ithaca, with one of his heaviest markings, three emphatic lines in the margin:

> He bestowed
> A veil on truth; for evermore did wind
> About his bosom a most crafty mind [xiii. 370].

That scene, in which the slippery explanations of Odysseus are affectionately shown up by Athena, can be read as high comedy. If Melville did not read it so, and if this moment is one of the last he would underscore in the poem, it was not only because he felt as Lear's Fool felt (in a passage he checked elsewhere) that "Truth's a dog must to kennel." To suppose so would be to remember the markings while forgetting the poem. And I want to suggest that the markings and the poem together make a curious tension which is representative both of Melville's relation to tradition and of the operation of that relation in the best of his fiction.

Melville had perhaps the most strenuous doubts of his generation about the possibility of uttering the truth, and in his later years he was greatly taken by Arnold's allusion to the "power and beauty in the well-kept secret of one's self and one's thoughts." Here we find him, perhaps, attributing such beauty to the secretive Odysseus in Ithaca. But these doubts were embraced by a larger doubt which had to do with the nature of the truth to be uttered; and Melville was increasingly sure that truth was double—that it was dialectical and contained, so far as any poet could utter it, in a tension. In his reading of the *Odyssey*, Melville inserted a tension into the poem: the tension between his own tragic and truncated design—the departure, the journey of inquiry, the suffering, the secretiveness— and the grand pattern which the poem nonetheless maintains of homecoming, reunion, and resounding victory.

Melville's reading reinforces the sense we have of how any formal and formulated myth functions in *Moby-Dick* and afterward. What I have said about the *Odyssey* myth can be matched by his response to the Christian myth (if that is the right phrase for it), or to the tragedies of Aeschylus or Shakespeare. Bits and pieces or the whole of these myths are introduced into the narrative. But they are not precisely the model echoed in the central action, re-enacted by the main event. They are the known elements by a sort of bold breach- ing of which the incident or the character or the phrase or the whole action must be understood. Yet the mythic elements are not negated either. They serve to comment contrapuntally on the action and the hero, which, of course, comment in turn upon them: and this is how the figures on both sides become transfigured.

The process is not always radiant in Melville, for the traditional materials appear raggedly, they are lumpy and not altogether digested; there is hardly a doctrinaire theory behind their treat- ment. A much clearer example in recent fiction is the functioning of *The Divine Comedy* in Thomas Mann's *The Magic Mountain*. When, for instance, Hans Castorp's second "guide," Naphta, chal- lenges the young man's first "guide," Settembrini, to a duel and then kills himself, we are meant to hear the almost endless dis- cordant vibrations set up by the contrast between this event and the relation, in the *Comedy*, of Dante's guides—Virgil (whom Settembrini cherishes and resembles) and Beatrice (like Naphta, a theologian). The relation between Virgil and Beatrice is perfectly harmonious; it enacts, indeed, the process toward perfection; it dramatizes the formula of St. Thomas that grace does not destroy nature but perfects it. The harmonious hum of the *Comedy* behind the pistol-shots of *The Magic Mountain* establishes the tension: a tension of symbolic relationships, which is a tension of worlds; and the world of Mann's novel announces itself in its ironic contrast to Dante's.

Nothing so crafty or so conscious may be found in the fiction of Melville; yet the achievement is comparable. And even the lumpiness of the traditional elements included is significant: significant, anyhow, that his relation to the tradition was American. For the American writer has never (if he is honest and American) been able to pretend an authentic initial communion with the European past; and especially not if he begins, as Melville did, imbued with the antitraditional principles of the party of Hope. He can know a great deal, even everything, about that past; he can go after it, which is just the demonstration that he is not in communion with it. And if he establishes a communion, it is one of a quite different order from that which most European writers — until 1939, at least — possessed as their birthright. The American kind of communion will usually be a sort of tussle, and the best of our writers (like Melville) can convert the tussle into drama. At the same time, since the American writer is outside the organic world of European literature to start with, there is no limit to how much of the world he can draw upon. He has the Protestant's contempt for the long line of commentary and influence; he can go directly to the source and find it anywhere. Nothing is his by right; and so nothing constrains him; and nothing, ultimately, is denied him. Such has been and such must continue to be the actual relation between the American writer and the European tradition: a queer and vigilant relation, at once hospitable and hostile, at once unlimited and uneasy.[2]

---

[2]Cf. the discussion of "communion" in chap. 9, and especially in the closing pages of that chapter. "Communion" — or the attempt to achieve it — is, I suggest there, a link between the various members of what I call "the third party": the elder James, Bushnell, Hawthorne, Melville, Parkman, etc. Cf. also the mention on p. 160 of the American loss of "communion with history."

H. Bruce Franklin

[*Moby-Dick* as Myth]

In the chapter "Moby Dick," historical, psychological, metaphysical, and moral truth all meet in the myth of the White Whale, the myth serving, as it serves throughout the book, to mediate these several kinds of myth. The chapter defines more extensively than any other chapter Moby Dick's history, what he represents to the minds of men, and what he symbolizes philosophically and morally. Yet it tells practically nothing of the whale that is not, at least in the most general sense, mythical. The whale's history is as dubious, as equivocal, and as mysterious as his divinity and his malignancy. The entire chapter, while continually defining the myth of Moby Dick, continually insists that the myth is mythical. Almost every detail of his history is questioned as it is presented. Only his physical appearance, his ferocity, and the fact that he encountered Ahab are not to be questioned. Behind and beyond this is mystery. His physical attributes are most uncertain and possibly supernatural, his attacks may be the workings of either a brutish ferocity or some

Reprinted from *The Wake of the Gods: Melville's Mythology*, by H. Bruce Franklin, pp. 54-61, with the permission of the publishers, Stanford University Press. © 1963 by the Board of Trustees of the Leland Stanford Junior University.

mysteriously "intelligent malignity," and the number and nature of these attacks are, possibly, extraordinary. The most well-seasoned Melville reader may be the very one to overlook much of the equivocation, for he may assume that double negatives, the passive voice, involuted syntax, and a hesitant wording signal a most important and most positive assertion. He might, for instance, assume that this positively asserts the whale's intelligent malignity:

> But though similar disasters, however little bruited ashore, *were by no means unusual* in the fishery; yet, *in most instances,* such *seemed* the White Whale's infernal aforethought of ferocity, that *every* dismembering or death that he caused, was *not wholly* regarded as having been inflicted by an *unintelligent* agent. [Italics mine.]

If this asserts anything positively, it asserts positive doubt. Yet the whale's intelligent malignity is his most important nonphysical attribute, and in another context would be by no means far-fetched. The wilder suggestions about Moby Dick, although they prove extremely important to understanding the book, are qualified and equivocated even more. This equivocation lies at the heart of *Moby-Dick,* partly because the heart of Moby Dick is the central mystery in a world of mysteries.

In a world of mysteries, myths become of almost ultimate importance. But myths, as mythologists of all ages have discovered, are themselves perhaps the most puzzling of mysteries. All this is true in the world of *Moby-Dick. Moby-Dick* displays truth as a collection of mysteries, dramatizes these mysteries as myths, and uses Western comparative mythology from sources as varied as Plutarch, David Hume, the Reverend Thomas Maurice, and the *North American Review* to help examine these myths.

Besides allegorical, etymological, and religious explanations, there have always been two basic explanations of myth. When formalized, these two major schools of mythological theory have opposed each other in Western thought at least since the fifth century before Christ—the historical and the psychological. (Like most distinctions, those which separate these two schools exist more in theory than in fact. But these theoretic distinctions have their usefulness.) Myth, by definition, cannot be history. Myths may be events of human and natural history as they are distorted, fictionalized, or allegorized by the mind. Or myths may be events of the mind as they are dramatized in narrative form, that is, in terms of natural or historical events. In either case, they are products of the interaction of psychological processes and external reality, combining something of both psychological events and historical or natural events. The distinction which I am going to make between the "historical" and the "psychological" schools is this: the historical school assumes that myth is natural or human history veiled by psychology; it seeks to remove that veil and to discover historical truth. The psychological school assumes that myth is psychology veiled by its narrative formulation; it seeks to remove that veil and to discover psychological truth. The two schools thus agree that myth equals history plus psychology but disagree about the relative importance of the two ingredients. Returning to *Mardi,* we can compare Sir William Jones and Melville in terms of this working distinction. Jones is as good a specimen as one finds of the historical school; Melville, although he admits and dramatizes Jones's theories, overrides these theories with psychological concerns and ultimately enrolls himself in the psychological school. Jones lists four ways in which the human mind, by distorting external reality, produces mythology. The historian perverts history perhaps to curry favor with his king, ignorant awe makes a people personify astronomical objects and events, poets plant nymphs in nature to entertain, and philosophers incarnate their metaphysics in the physical world. Jones seeks to restore what he considers historical and natural truth, the truth of the Judaic-Christian revelation. Melville dramatizes the mythologizing described by Jones, but he turns from the thing distorted — external reality, which remains an enigma — to the distorter, human psychology. Jones finds that myth yields an absolute truth about its ultimate object, God, who fashions and truly reveals history and nature. Melville suggests that the only ultimate truth that myth yields is a truth about its ultimate source, the human mind.

In the chapter "Moby Dick" these two ways of looking at myth are related with great precision and great complexity. The history of Moby Dick is related to the myth of Moby Dick exactly as typical contemporaneous works of comparative mythology of the historical school related history to myth. One of the favorite phenomena of the eighteenth- and nineteenth-century historical school was known as the "Asiatic" or "Oriental" imagination. With one hand, the apologists could explain any differences between the Bible and current archaeology, geology, paleontology, biology, astronomy, or Common Sense by pointing to the "Oriental style" of the transcribers of Scripture; with the other hand, they could wave off other scriptures as mere products of the "Oriental imagination." The skeptics, of course, were using both hands to combine the tricks; the Bible was only one more collection of the fantastic products of the Oriental imagination, which, for both groups, was a compound of ignorance, superstition, and fancy overblown by a hot climate and wild geography. Melville's substitute for the Oriental imagination is the whaleman's imagination — something even wilder than the common seaman's imagination — and he offers it as the explanation of those "wild rumors of all sorts" which did not "fail to exaggerate, and still the more horrify the true histories of these deadly encounters":

> For not only do fabulous rumors naturally grow out of the very body of all surprising terrible events . . . but, in maritime life, far more than in that of terra firma, wild rumors abound, wherever there is any adequate reality for them to cling to. And as the sea surpasses the land in this matter, so the whale fishery surpasses every other sort of maritime life, in the wonderfulness and fearfulness of the rumors which sometimes circulate there. For not only are whalemen as a body unexempt from that ignorance and superstitiousness hereditary to all sailors; but of all sailors, they are by all odds the most directly brought into contact with whatever is appallingly astonishing in the sea . . . the whaleman is wrapped by influences all tending to make his fancy pregnant with many a mighty birth.
>
> No wonder, then, that ever gathering volume from the mere transit over the widest watery spaces, the outblown rumors of the White Whale did in the end incorporate with themselves all manner of morbid hints, and half-formed foetal suggestions of supernatural agencies, which eventually invested Moby Dick with new terrors unborrowed from anything that visibly appears.

What may have been a direct source for this passage, David Hume's *Natural History of Religion*, defines part of what Melville is here doing:

> The absurdity [of anthropomorphism] is not less, while we cast our eyes upwards; and transferring, as is too usual, human passions and infirmities to the deity, represent him as jealous and revengeful, capricious and partial, and, in short, a wicked and foolish man, in every respect but his superior power and authority. No wonder, then, that mankind, being placed in such an absolute ignorance of causes, and being at the same time so anxious concerning their future fortune, should immediately acknowledge a dependence on invisible powers, possessed of sentiment and intelligence. . . .
>
> In proportion as any man's course of life is governed by accident, we always find, that he increases in superstition; as may particularly be observed of gamesters and sailors, who, though, of all man-

kind, the least capable of serious reflection, abound most in frivolous and superstitious apprehensions.

Melville, like Hume, is showing how the human imagination projects itself into the inscrutable physical world, transforming inscrutability into mythic religion. Unlike Hume, however, he takes seriously the most superstitious, unsubstantial, nonphysical, and supernatural rumors, hints, and suggestions.

Before presenting these rumors, hints, and suggestions, Melville points out that similar things "in former legendary times" had been thought about the Sperm Whale in general, an object of great superstitious dread. Finally, the suggestions are made, and very important suggestions to *Moby-Dick* they prove to be — the ubiquity in time and space of the White Whale. But these suggestions are offered only as the distortion of historical truth by ignorance, fear, and superstition, represented by the whaleman's imagination:

> One of the *wild suggestings* referred to, as at last *to be linked* with the White Whale *in the minds of the superstitiously inclined,* was the *unearthly conceit* that Moby Dick was ubiquitous...
> Nor, *credulous* as such minds must have been, was this *conceit altogether without some faint show of superstitious* probability....
> ... it cannot be much matter of surprise that *some whalemen* should go still further in their *superstitions*; declaring Moby Dick not only ubiquitous, but immortal... [Italics mine.]

We may tend to accept Moby Dick's ubiquity in time and space, but we should never forget that this ubiquity is dubious in so far as it is presented as historical truth. Nonetheless it is ultimately of the greatest truth. Although perhaps not historical fact, it is a psychological and hence a metaphysical and moral fact, and a very real, very important fact. Since historical truth cannot be known, other truths prevail.

Here, as in *Mardi*, Melville confronts the epistemological dead end, retraces his steps, and heads in a different direction. The historical truth about the White Whale, like the historical truth about Alma's avatar, is unknowable. But the psychological truth about the White Whale's ubiquity, his intelligent malignity, and his demonism can, like the psychological truth about the revelations of Alma, be known. The most important passage in *Moby-Dick* is the one which presents the psychological truth of the White Whale:

Small reason was there to doubt, then, that ever since that almost fatal encounter, Ahab had cherished a wild vindictiveness against the whale, all the more fell for that in his frantic morbidness he at last came to identify with him, not only all his bodily woes, but all his intellectual and spiritual exasperations. The White Whale swam before him as the monomaniac incarnation of all those malicious agencies which some deep men feel eating in them, till they are left living on with half a heart and half a lung. The intangible malignity which has been from the beginning; to whose dominion even the modern Christians ascribe one-half of the worlds; which the ancient Ophites of the east reverenced in their statue devil; — Ahab did not fall down and worship it like them; but deliriously transferring its idea to the abhorred white whale, he pitted himself, all mutilated, against it. All that most maddens and torments; all that stirs up the lees of things; all truth with malice in it; all that cracks the sinews and cakes the brain; all the subtle demonisms of life and thought; all evil, to crazy Ahab, were visibly personified, and made practically assailable in Moby Dick. He piled upon the whale's white hump the sum of all the general rage and hate felt by his whole race from Adam down; and then, as if his chest had been a mortar, he burst his hot heart's shell upon it.

Ahab's madness turns the wild fantasies of the whaleman's imagination into psychological, metaphysical, and moral fact. Moby Dick's ubiquity in time and his malignity, so equivocal in the whalemen's legends, are certainty to Ahab; he assumes without question "that intangible malignity which has been from the beginning." And his madness combines with the whaleman's imagination, embodied by the *Pequod's* crew, to create a myth which determines the fate of both captain and crew.

In a world in which historical truth is attainable, Ahab's insanity would be defined as the difference between the real world and the world of Ahab's mind. But in the external world of *Moby-Dick* the White Whale's historical truth consists merely in visible objects which are but as pasteboard masks. Ahab's mind is free to define Moby Dick. This is not to say that Ahab's psychological truth is the only possible psychological truth. There is indeed a tension between Ahab's psychological truth and, say, Starbuck's. When, however, Starbuck's "soul" is "overmanned" by "a madman," the White Whale is defined not only as Ahab's "intellectual and spiritual exasperations," but as "all evil . . . visibly personified." The crew sees the whale through Ahab's mind: they share his hate, his enemy, and his pursuit; Ishmael abandons his mind to Ahab's,

though in Moby Dick he can see "naught but the deadliest ill."
Since the *Pequod's* polyglot crew, that "Anacharsis Clootz deputa-
tion," represents all mankind, the fact that Ahab's psychological
truth becomes theirs is of utmost significance. When Ahab's mind
speaks to theirs, and their minds, as one, echo his, their enemy
appears as a monster from the mind:

> How it was that they so aboundingly responded to the old man's
> ire — by what evil magic their souls were possessed, that at times
> his hate seemed almost theirs; the White Whale as much their in-
> sufferable foe as his; how all this came to be — what the White
> Whale was to them, or how to their unconscious understandings,
> also, in some dim, unsuspected way, he might have seemed the glid-
> ing great demon of the seas of life, — all this to explain, would be to
> dive deeper than Ishmael can go.

These terms locate the action of *Moby-Dick* within the area of
modern psychological theories of mythology, a stream which has
been growing steadily from Bayle to Hume to Jung. With no system
and no jargon, Melville penetrates deeply enough to reveal the
psychological truth of the White Whale. Ahab, by reaching the
unconscious understandings of the crew, succeeds in piling "upon
the whale's white hump the sum of all the general rage and hate
felt by his whole race." He succeeds in evoking a myth, succeeds
in completing the formula of one of Melville's mythologically
oriented literary contemporaries: "In the mythus a superhuman
intelligence uses the unconscious thoughts and dreams of men as
its hieroglyphics." Ahab succeeds in fashioning Moby Dick into
"the gliding great demon of the seas of life."

4. The Candles

Emilio Cecchi

[A Note] on Melville

Moby Dick (1931)

While a great many American authors put forward a more or less conventional and Europeanized picture of the birth of their civilization, Melville takes us right back to the poetry of its origin, and wallows in the fundamental concept of nineteenth century America, the idea of the contrast between man and nature, a nature constantly subdued and yet unvanquished. The wild story of Captain Ahab sailing the ocean in pursuit of Moby Dick, the white whale, the huge and fierce Leviathan, is made to correspond to the myths which lie at the origin of history: to the "heroic and chivalric tales" to which Vico alludes, to Hercules fighting the Hydra and the lion, to Theseus killing the Minotaur and to Perseus slaying the sea-monster.

But the ancients, whose experience and conception of nature was narrow, were content to symbolize its power and terror in forms which held little or nothing of grandeur. The moderns, who have subdued nature to an extent which would have seemed utopia to

From "Two Notes on Melville," *Sewanee Review*, LXVIII (July-September, 1960), 398-406.

our forbears, have an immense respect for the force of nature just in proportion as their power of domination is great. Moby Dick and all the creatures that people the depths, the whole life of the sea, are represented by Melville with a solemn gravity that at times seems almost to carry us into a geological era before the appearance of man. These are no longer the made-up, artificial monsters, magnificent in their childishness, in which the imagination of the Greeks sought to portray a hostile and incomprehensible nature.

And again: in ancient pictures and statues Hercules, Theseus, Perseus and St. George tower over their bestial and hellish antagonists. Dragons and hydras are knee-high. This stature, while it gives man an air of triumph, at the same time takes something of drama from his exploit and his victory. But Ahab and his crew are like pygmies attacking a living mountain. Hercules, Theseus and the Red Cross Knights have an Olympus or Paradise from which the divinity looks down and supports them like a father. Ahab has nothing but his own obstinacy, his heroic madness, he measures himself against the colossi not for any earthly or heavenly prize to reward his perils and labors, but because this is the law that man has laid down for himself. He wins more than Hercules and Theseus had won, but in the end he is beaten, because he set himself to win more than was possible, knowing that he was sacrificing himself to the attempt.

And the story of the white whale is typically American also in its literary form. As America is an agglomeration of races and traditions from which a new race and tradition has been formed, so in this book the material is gathered from widely differing cultures, and reflects the most varied spiritual interests and levels of taste, yet is nevertheless fused by a new heat, unified by a new accent. At one moment we seem to be reading a scientific and scholarly work on the whale, at another a grim Puritanical commentary on the verses in *Job* and *Isaiah* which speak of the Leviathans of the hoary deep. Sometimes there is a passage of imaginative erudition in the style of Sir Thomas Browne, then a ribald conversation after the manner of Rabelais, or a shaft of satire worthy of Swift. But the whole work has a tone of its own, and a breathless and colossal vitality. There is nothing that echoes the cloying enthusiasms of Longfellow, or the slightly confused humanitarianism of Whitman, and nothing of the sketch-book humor in which Bret Harte and others made light of the achievement of the pioneers. *Moby Dick* is an angry, gloomy, Faust-like book, so that men have found no better remedy than the one applied to a very different work,

Gulliver's Travels, which was written to stir them up to even greater depths: they pretend that it is no more than a story for children.

Melville's work is an extremely lively and complex document of the American spirit, in the tumultuous labor of its formation. His book has all the qualities of violence. And his superb mysticism will never age, even if the eighty years that have run since Melville wrote have been so rich in events as to make him seem to belong not so much to historic as to prehistoric America.

Cesare Pavese

The Literary Whaler (1923)

The importance today of Herman Melville, the nineteenth-century writer who is only now returning to fame, can be considered in a contrast; we, the descendants of the nineteenth century, have in our bones that taste for adventure, for the primitive, and for real life which is the aftermath of culture, freeing us from complications, providing a balm to the plague sores of decadence, to the diseases of civilization. The names of our heroes are still Rimbaud, Gauguin and Stevenson, while Herman Melville instead lived first through real adventures, through the primitive state. He was first a barbarian and then, later, he entered the world of culture and thought, bringing with him the sanity and balance he had acquired in the life he had been leading. It is clear that for some time we have been feeling a growing need for a return to barbarity. This can be seen from the increasing popularity of travel, of sport, of films and of jazz, from the interest in Negroes and from a hundred other signs which it seems banal to recall and which we label as anti-literary. All this is doubtless very fine. But it is the manner which offends. It seems to me that, in this anti-literary frenzy, there is a tendency

From *Sewanee Review*, LXVIII (Summer, 1960), 407-418.

towards a primitivism bordening on imbecility. Imbecility, or rather, weakness: it is cowardly to take refuge from the complications of life in an over-simplified paradise which, after all, is only another of the many refinements of civilization. I was wrong before: our hero is not Rimbaud, or Gauguin or Stevenson, it is the wreck of a man. Melville's ideal, on the other hand, is Ishmael, a sailor who can row half a day behind a whale with his illiterate companions, and then retire to a masthead to meditate on Plato.

It is not for nothing that Melville is a North American. We have much to learn in this connection from these newcomers in the field of culture, who have been held responsible by its defenders, not without justice, though without blame, for the return of our ideals to barbarism. The Americans for their part discovered how to re-invigorate culture, sieving it through primitive and actual experience, not like us, by substituting one term for another, but by enriching, modifying and strengthening literature through what is called life.

That a thought has no meaning unless it is thought by the whole man is an American concept, and this is the ideal toward which the whole of the literature of the United States, from Thoreau to Sherwood Anderson, either consciously or unconsciously aims. It created powerful individuals, passing a good many years in a barbarous state, living and absorbing, and then dedicating themselves to culture, and presenting the reality which they had known in thoughts and images that had something of the harmony we associate with the Greeks. This is a far cry from the artificial paradises situated at the ends of the earth in which our own fastidious neo-barbarians make their return to nature. . . .

Melville was a true Greek. Reading European evasions of literature makes you feel more literary than ever; you feel tiny, cerebral, effeminate; reading Melville, who was not ashamed to begin *Moby Dick*, his poem of barbarous life, with eight pages of quotations and to go on by discussing, quoting again, and being the man of letters, you expand your lungs, you enlarge your brain, you feel more alive and more of a man. And though *Moby Dick*, like Greek tragedy, may be dark and gloomy, yet the serenity and clarity of the chorus (Ishmael) is so great that you leave the theatre each time with a sense of increased vitality. . . .

It is necessary to have a clear idea of what Melville's culture, the culture which plays so large a part in his works, consists of. It would be a mistake to believe that this man had an eighteenth century training. For him, as for the whole literary world of the

United States between the years of 1830-1850 (Poe, Emerson, Hawthorne, Alcott, etc.) the eighteenth century, although very well known, had been left behind, at least in its most typically eighteenth century aspects. Benjamin Franklin no longer interested anyone except the patriots. The tastes of this "golden age" are close to the tastes of the English poets Coleridge, Keats and Shelley; the great century for them is the seventeenth century which includes a good half of the sixteenth century as well. Yet, while Keats or Shelley were looking to the early seventeenth century mainly for a lyrical and stylistic tradition, the North Americans, and Melville above all, found deeper roots, not only in the memories of the historical crises from which their colony originated, but in the need they felt to recall the proud thirst for spiritual liberty, for the unknown and for the distant land which gave life and traditions to this colony.

These New Englanders were great Bible readers (and, it should be remembered, the authorized version dates from 1611). In *Moby Dick* the Bible is to be felt at every step, not only in the sound of the names of Ahab, Ishmael, Rachel, Jeroboam, Bildad, Elijah and the rest, but in the constant presence of a spirit of Puritan awe and severity, turning what might have been a scientific tale of terror in the Poe tradition into a dark moral tragedy, where the catastrophe is brought about not by human or natural forces but by a monster known as the leviathan.

The curious fact is that Melville retained an unprejudiced rationalistic attitude towards the Bible. In *Moby Dick* there is a highly amusing chapter on "Jonah historically regarded." And this is where the seventeenth century really comes in.

At the same time the lively tone of the new scientific and philosophic terminology which was in the process of formation, mixing together solemn Latinisms with nervous, almost vernacular, expressions of the new sensibility, is often re-echoed in the pages of the Puritan whaler. If I could be certain that he had read him, I should say that Melville took more from Giordano Bruno than from anyone. But these are thorny questions. In any case the writers with which he can most justifiably be connected are Rabelais and the Elizabethans, in whom the same love of catalogues, of verbal profusion and of *vivez joyeux* are present. At times Melville even reaches the point of introducing burlesque quotations. And the Elizabethans gave him the dazzling style, those thick-piled images, that love of contrasts which is however, in the end a mark of over facility of imagination. But the current at which Melville drank most deeply, which lies at the roots of all seventeenth century thought, was Platonizing rationalism, especially the rationalism of the English essayists. Naturally, as with the Bible, he read Plato, and, I imagine, the Neoplatonists and the mystics, from beginning to end. But the historical guise in which these tendencies appeared to him was undoubtedly that of the English seventeenth century. Thomas Browne was not only his teacher of style, but his spiritual father, and the sentence of *Religio Medici* ". . . that this visible World is but a Picture of the invisible, wherein, as in a Pourtraict, things are not truely, but in equivocal shapes . . ." is not only to be found again in the epigraph to Coleridge's *Ballad of the Ancient Mariner*—another essential clue to the understanding of *Moby Dick*—but it returns once more in the latter work on the lips of Captain Ahab, who (mad though he was) belonged to the same philosophical school as the author. Now Thomas Browne, besides being a sort of mystic magician, is also a subtle rationalist, and puts forward certain arguments for the Christian religion that have led rigid doctrinaires to take him for a heretic or an atheist.

Such was Melville's attitude. In his early books about Polynesia —*Typee* (1846) and *Omoo* (1847)—and in *White Jacket* (1850), he is still a strong young man who loves the wind and the sun and the beautiful native girls and adventures with happy endings: he is, we might say, still unaware. But if you open *Mardi* (1848) and finally *Moby Dick* (1851) you find the wider experience of a man tortured by insoluble doubts, driving him, in *Mardi*, into curious allegorical confusions, and in *Moby Dick*, into a few exasperated declamations; but, above all, to a lucid and subtle investigation, to a scientific examination, meditation and continuous quotation, in order to solve the mystery.

Melville is no quack who makes use of a halo of mystery every time he wants to produce an effect and does not know what to say. He is one of the doubting Thomases who are to be found precisely in the seventeenth century. As the Apostles would not believe in the Resurrection, Melville in *Moby Dick* does not want to believe in the breathless phantom, one of the supernatural effects hinted at; he does not want to believe that Fedallah, the head of Ahab's Malays, has such an odor of brimstone about him; he does not want to believe in omens, and even tries to explain away the shoals which follow Ahab's boat by the fact that sharks prefer the flesh of Malays to any other. The mystery which remains in *Moby Dick:* the demonism of the universe, the conscious power which underlies natural destructive forces, the invisible world of which the visible is but a picture, this is a real mystery (given Melville's peculiar turn of thought) and a critic allowing rein to his imagination might say that the fate of Captain Ahab awaits whoever tries to solve this mystery. . . .

As with all great works, you never get to the end of *Moby Dick;* you discover new points of view, new meanings and new values.

I have already mentioned what seems to me to be the deepest meaning of the story, but in spite of this, how much the reader has still to learn from its austere legendary tone, from that style which, above and beyond its wealth of fantasy, is pregnant with strict moral thought. Or from the tense and solemn pace, accompanied at times by a mischievous smile, with which the chapters of realistic description, information and discussion, proceed. But above all it is the constant sense of the enormous, of the superhuman, toward which the whole book converges, in a miracle of construction by which little by little the gay and puritanical atmosphere of the beginning and the learned atmosphere of the long explanations of the central passages are finally blended in a spirit of conscious and daring action which is almost mythical, as the name and fame of the White Whale, which only appears toward the end of the book, grow until they seem gigantic and occupy all places, all actions and all thoughts. . . .

W. H. Auden

Ishmael-Melville

Ishmael cannot properly be called a member of the crew; for, from the moment that he steps on board, he only speaks or is spoken to once more when after his first ducking (baptism) he makes his will, i.e., consciously accepts the absolute finality of his commitment. From then on, he becomes simply the recording consciousness, the senses and the mind through which we experience everything.

This suggests that if we are identified with him then, we should also identify ourselves with him during the prologue when he does have a certain personal existence.

One day in Manhattan Ishmael resolves to go whaling. To this resolution he is pushed from behind by the need to escape from a spiritual condition of spleen and powerlessness — Manhattan is for him the *selva oscura* of the *Divine Comedy* and the Sargasso Sea of the Ancient Mariner; and he is lured from in front by a vague but haunting image. He has never consciously heard of Moby Dick yet:

From *The Enchaféd Flood,* by W. H. Auden, pp. 115-124. Copyright 1950 by The Rector and Visitors of the University of Virginia. Reprinted by permission of Random House, Inc.

in the wild conceits that swayed me to my purpose, two and two
there floated into my inmost soul, endless processions of the whale,
and, midmost of them all, one grand hooded phantom, like a snow
hill in the air.

But between this initial resolve and the actual decision, the
irrevocable commitment of signing on the *Pequod*, he has a preliminary journey to make, during which he is subjected to various
initiations from any of which he could draw back and return to
the city.

He begins to move away from the safe centre of normal routine,
convention and status (he has been a schoolmaster, i.e., a conventional authority) towards the edge of the land to the port New
Bedford. The first test is a shock of fright. Imagining it to be an
inn, i.e., a place of shelter and friendly companionship, he pushes
open the door of *The Trap* and finds himself in a Negro church
when the minister is preaching about hell, the wailing and gnashing
of teeth. This is a warning that in his state of spleen from which
he is trying to escape, it is easy to take a wrong turning — into
despair. He rejects this and enters the Spouter Inn whose proprietor
has the ominous name of Coffin. (It is finally a coffin that saves
him from drowning — death and rebirth are two aspects of the same
thing. Who would save his life must lose it.) Here he has a brief
glimpse of the Handsome Sailor, Bulkington, who will play no part
in *Moby Dick*, but will appear as a protagonist in a later work of
Melville's under the name of Billy Budd, and the whole Queequeg
episode begins.

Ishmael is a white man and a Presbyterian: Queequeg is a
South-Sea Islander and a Pagan, formerly a cannibal. The Christian
world is the world of consciousness, i.e., the ethically superior world
which knows the truth, both the artistic and scientific truths and
the moral truth that one should love one's neighbor as oneself.

The pagan world is the unconscious world, which does not know
the truth. The cannibalism it practises is a symbol of self-love, of
treating one's neighbor as existing solely for one's own advantage.
Queequeg left his island in order to become conscious of the truth,
only to discover that those who are conscious of it do not obey it,
and so has decided to live as a pagan in the Christian world.

Ishmael, like us, has two preconceived notions.
1) That men who are not white are ugly, i.e., in a physical sense,
   aesthetically inferior. He has just had that notion reinforced by
   seeing the handsome white Bulkington.

2) That pagans cannot obey the Christian commandment to love one's neighbor as oneself, because they have never heard the Word of the true God, i.e., they are ethically inferior.

Ishmael is disabused of both notions. He admits that Queequeg is beautiful, and that he loves his neighbor, in fact, more than most Christians. When on the short voyage from New Bedford to Nantucket Queequeg rescues from drowning — again a test of Ishmael's courage (can he face the possibility of drowning?) — the man who has just insulted him, saying "It's a mutual joint-stock world in all meridians. We cannibals must help these Christians," he exhibits Christian forgiveness and Christian *agape* without the slightest effort. He is a doer of the Word who has never heard the Word.

By accepting Queequeg — the symbolic act of acceptance is his joining in the worship of Queequeg's idol — Ishmael proves himself worthy of the voyage.

The last tests are the mysterious warning by Elijah not to sail on the *Pequod*, another test of courage, and the encounter with the owners, Captains Peleg and Bildad.

This pair are Quakers, i.e., people who consciously believe in applying the absolute law of love in time and the world. No man who is not a saint can do this; Ishmael has first to be made conscious through this pair of the discrepancy between Heaven's time and Jerusalem time, and then to be warned against falling into either of the two temptations which follow the moment one is so conscious, either of frivolity, i.e., taking the contradiction too lightly, which is what Peleg does, or, more seriously, of hypocrisy, i.e., of pretending that there is no contradiction and that one is living by Heaven's time, which is what Bildad does. Bildad's besetting vice is avarice, which is the spiritual version of cannibalism. He does not eat men, but he exploits them to the death. Avarice is worse than cannibalism because the latter is limited by natural appetite — you cannot eat more than a certain amount of flesh — but avarice has no limits — there is no end to the accumulation of money.

Father Mapple's Sermon

Standing apart from Ishmael's other tests is Father Mapple's Sermon. This is not, as has sometimes been said, a magnificent irrelevance, but an essential clue to the meaning of the whole book. The story of Jonah is the story of a voyage undertaken for the wrong reasons, of learning repentance through suffering and a final acceptance of duty. Jonah has ethical authority, i.e., he knows the Word; he is called upon to become more than that, to become an ethical hero with absolute passion, i.e., a religious hero; he flees from the divine command out of aesthetic pride, a fear that he will not be listened to and admired, not be an aesthetic hero. He is punished for his refusal by being confronted with the really aesthetically great, the storm and the whale, compared with which the greatest emperor is a puny weakling, and then, in the whale's belly, he is deprived of even the one gift he had, his ability to hear the Word. Humbled, he does not despair but repents and trusts in the God whom he can no longer hear. God forgives him, he is cast up on the land, and sets off to fulfill his vocation.

In drawing the moral, Father Mapple says two apparently contradictory things.
1) If we obey God, we must disobey ourselves; and it is in this disobeying of ourselves, wherein the hardness of obeying God consists.
2) Delight is to him — a far, far upward and inward delight — who against the proud gods and commodores of this earth ever stands forth his own inexorable self.

This is the same thing that the Button-Moulder says to Peer Gynt:

> To be one's self is to slay one's self
> But as perhaps that explanation
> Is thrown away on you, let's say,
> To follow out, in everything,
> What the Master's intention was. (v. 9.)

Man's being is a copulative relation between a subject ego and a predicate self. The ego is aware of the self as given, already there in the world, finite, derived, along with, related and comparable to other beings. It is further aware of the self not only as existing but also as potential, as not fully actual but as a self which becomes itself.

Being of itself unaware of its potentialities, the self cannot become itself of itself, cannot initiate anything; all it desires is to be in equilibrium, a self-enjoying, self-sufficient self: the responsibility for self-realisation lies with the ego which can decide; the self can only welcome or resist the decision when it is taken.

The ego, on the other hand, has no potentialities, only existence. Further, it is isolated; it cannot compare its egoship with other egos, as it can compare the self it is related to with other selves.

The desire of the ego is a double one. As freely owning a self, it desires a self of which it can approve. As solitary it desires to be approved of for the self it has. This approval must have absolute authority, for the approval of finite beings whom the ego can see are not self-existent posits an ultimate authority which approves of their approval, i.e., the ego desires a God.

The ego, therefore, has three tasks:

1) To know the self and the world, as they exist now.
2) To know the true God and what He requires the ego to realise in the self as he knows it.
3) To obey these commands.

The ego may err in three ways:

1) It may refuse to look honestly at its given self and prefer a vague or a fantastic conception to the truth. The temptation to do so arises from the fear that if it should know the truth about the self, it would find that it had a self of which it did not approve, i.e., not the sort of self it would like to have to develop.
2) It may prefer a false god to the true God. The temptation to do this arises out of a fear that if it knew the true God, the ego would encounter disapproval. A false god or idol is always one which the ego believes it can manage through magic; upon whose approval, therefore, it can, if it is smart enough, depend.
3) Knowing the self and what God requires to realise in the self, it may disobey negatively out of weakness, yielding to the opposition of the self to change, or positively out of defiance, in assertion of its autonomy.

The Voyage of The Pequod

The voyage of the *Pequod* is one voyage for Ishmael and with him us, and another for the rest of the crew.

For us the voyage signifies the exploration of the self and the world, of potential essences. Nothing happens to us, we survive, and we are the same people at the end as at the beginning except that we know ourselves and others better. We had to be tested first to see whether we were capable of such an exploration; once we have passed the tests, we have nothing to do but record.

For the rest of the crew, however, it is not the voyage of self-inspection before the act, but the act of historical existence itself. They learn nothing about themselves, but they are changed before our eyes, and reveal themselves unwittingly in what they say and do.

When we have finished the book, we realise why Father Mapple's sermon was put in where it was: in order that we might know the moral presuppositions by which we are to judge the speeches and actions of Ahab and the rest.

The crew of the *Pequod* are a society whose function is to kill whales. As such each has a specialised function of his own, arranged in a hierarchy of authority.

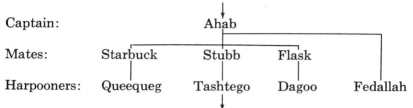

Captain: Ahab

Mates: Starbuck   Stubb   Flask

Harpooners: Queequeg   Tashtego   Dagoo   Fedallah

Then the crowd of seamen who man the whale-boats, of whom one or two appear for a moment, such as the old Manx sailor. Standing apart from them because their special functions are only indirectly connected with whales are:

> Pip, Ahab's cabin boy
> Perth, the Blacksmith
> Carpenter

In their motives for going on the voyage:

> Ahab wants to kill one particular whale.
> The Blacksmith wishes to escape his memories.
> The Carpenter wants to carpenter.

Pip doesn't want to go because he is terrified, but has no option. The rest have a common motive which makes them a community, they want to earn their living, in a way for which they are fitted and which they enjoy. Since they are doing what they like and are good at they are a happy community, and for them killing whales is morally permissible and indeed a much better job than most. It may sometimes tempt to unnecessary cruelty — as when Flask deliberately pricks the abscess of the old whale — but it encourages courage and democratic comradeship — the atmosphere on the *Pequod* is very different from that of the *Neversink*.

They are therefore in the right in going on the voyage. The only ones who should not have gone are firstly Ahab, because he has passed beyond killing whales in general, and secondly Pip, who lacks the courage which for whaling is essential, just as Captain De Deer of the *Jungfrau* and the captain of the *Rosebud* lack the necessary knowledge and skill.

Marius Bewley

[*Moby-Dick* and Creative Force]

The experiences in which Ishmael participates on the Pequod are, in a sense, his. They constitute a kind of passion play for him from which he is almost literally resurrected in the Epilogue into new life. The opening paragraph indicates the problem that faces Ishmael, and to which the action of the novel brings a cosmic solution:

> Whenever I find myself growing grim about the mouth; whenever it is a damp drizzly November in my soul; whenever I find myself involuntarily pausing before coffin warehouses, and bringing up the rear of every funeral I meet; and especially whenever my hypos get such an upper hand of me, that it requires a strong moral principle to prevent me from deliberately stepping into the street, and methodically knocking people's hats off — then, I account it high time to get to sea as soon as I can.

Though so casually expressed, Ishmael's malaise as described here represents the essence of that despair, though then greatly

From *The Eccentric Design* (New York: Columbia University Press, 1959), pp. 206-210.

exaggerated, which overtook Melville in *Pierre* and *The Confidence Man*. But in *Moby Dick* there will be, as the opening paragraph indicates, no submission to it, but a vigorous resistance. The sea is the source of life in the world, and it is to the sea that Ishmael returns whenever he feels symptoms of this depression. Ishmael, then, hardly less than Ahab may be said to do, sets out on the voyage on a quest, but it is a different quest from Ahab's. It is a quest for spiritual health, a desire to enter into a new and deeper harmony with creation. Ishmael accepts the mystery of creation — particularly as embodied in Leviathan — which Ahab does not. Ishmael's attitude towards Moby Dick is one of respectful reverence and wonder, and although from time to time during the course of the Pequod's voyage Ishmael comes under the influence of Ahab's intellectual domination, such occasions are momentary.

From the very beginning, Moby Dick is not a symbol of evil to Ishmael, but a magnificent symbol of creation itself. Creation is not a pasteboard mask for Ishmael, to be broken through in some excess of spiritual pride, as it was for Ahab, whose attempt to penetrate visible creation, not through love but hatred, could only end in a material vision. The measure of Ishmael's contrast in this respect is given in the following passage. Ishmael is paying a visit to the whaling chapel in New Bedford:

> 'Methinks that in looking at things spiritual, we are too much like oysters observing the sun through water, and thinking that thick water the thinnest air. In fact, take my body who will, take it, I say, it is not me. And therefore three cheers for Nantucket; and come a stove boat and stove my body when they will, for stave my soul Jove himself cannot.'

We are sometimes inclined to lose sight of the elementary fact that the whole complex movement of *Moby Dick* originates in Ahab's inability to resign himself, after Ishmael's fashion as indicated here, to the loss of a leg. Ahab is guilty of that most democratic of sins — of denying hierarchy between the body and soul, eternal and temporal values. He can proceed from a severed limb to a condemned and guilty universe with the greatest of ease. We are back at John Quincy Adams once again, who discovered in Eli Whitney's cotton gin God's great betrayal of the world. Essentially, democracy is the denial of degree, and, by implication, of limit also. But the very principle of form is boundary and limitation. Thus, the democratic aspiration that would deny the hieratic element in cre-

ation ends in a monstrous negation. It is the very essence of formlessness.

The degrees of knowledge are the most important of all for they
most directly reflect the degrees of order and value in the spiritual
world. It is an important element in Ahab's comprehensive significance that, in Chapter CXVIII, 'The Quadrant', he symbolically
destroys the instrument of knowledge by which he should determine
his location—his place in creation, as it were:

> Then gazing at his quadrant, and handling, one after the other,
> its numerous cabalistical contrivances, he pondered again, and
> muttered: 'Foolish toy! babies' plaything of haughty Admirals, and
> Commodores, and Captains; the world brags of thee, of thy cun-
> ning and might; but what after all canst thou do, but tell the poor,
> pitiful point, where thou thyself happenst to be on this wide planet,
> and the hand that holds thee: no! not a jot more!'

The manner in which the official hierarchy of the navy is merged
here with the ordered knowledge for which the quadrant stands, is
worth noting. The importance of this chapter is generally recognized;
but there is still reason to insist that it is not science as such that
Ahab is rejecting here. Rather, it is the idea of degree. It is precisely
Ahab's *place* in the universe which he does not wish, indeed refuses,
to know. And it is only his *place* that the quadrant can tell, his place
with reference to the sun. Thus, the paradox of the democratic
dogma that refuses to recognize anything above it exists in its being
forced back on the degrees below: 'Curse thee, thou quadrant! ... no
longer will I guide my earthly way by thee; the level ship's compass,
and the level dead-recokoning, by log and by line; *these* shall conduct me, and show me my place on the sea.' Once the ordered framework that controlled and directed the political vision of John
Adams, Cooper, and even of Jefferson, is rejected, we are confronted
by a breed of nineteenth-century Titans whose offspring is ultimately degraded to the 'common man' of the twentieth century.

Ahab's attitude is the antithesis of life because it represents a
rejection of creation. The analysis of this attitude forms the main
substance of the novel, but its great formal achievement exists in
the beautiful way that Melville placed the action in an evaluative
perspective so that its final effect is one of positive affirmation. He
achieved this in two ways. First, he built up the symbol of Leviathan, layer on layer, so that it became one of the most magnificent
images in the language of the positive aspects of creation. Leviathan,

especially in his greatest role of the White Whale, is the affirmation of all that Ahab denies. The impact of this recognition on the imagination is the greater because, if Melville leads one towards it irresistibly, we yet make the discovery in the midst of all the gargantuan suffering of the whaling ground. We learn the triumph of life that the White Whale represents only because we come to it through such seas of death. This is the most deeply Christian note that Melville ever strikes.

Secondly, Melville achieved the evaluative perspective for the action of *Moby Dick* through his use of Ishmael, and particularly by means of his 'resurrection' in the Epilogue. Ishmael, as I said, enrolls in the crew because he himself wishes to recover spiritual health. The long voyage that is finally brought to its disastrous termination in the China Seas, to repeat an earlier remark, is a kind of long drawn out passion play for Ishmael, ending in his symbolical 'resurrection', from which he returns to life, as we may surmise, cured of that spiritual malady from which we see him suffering in the first chapter of the book.

The relevant portions of the novel which deal with this symbolic resurrection are Chapter CX, and the Epilogue. It will be recalled that Ishmael's cannibal friend Queequeg is for a time so grievously afflicted with fever during the course of the voyage that his life is despaired of. As he seems to be dying, the ship's carpenter is asked to construct a coffin for him. But after the coffin is built, Queequeg recovers. The coffin itself has been strongly constructed, and Queequeg decides to use it for a sea chest, in his leisure moments covering the lid of it with a fancy design:

> With a wild whimsiness, he now used his coffin for a sea-chest; and emptying into it his canvas bag of clothes, set them in order there. Many spare hours he spent, in carving the lid with all manner of grotesque figures and drawings; and it seemed that hereby he was striving, in his rude way, to copy parts of the twisted tattooing on his body. And this tattooing had been a work of a departed prophet and seer of his island, who, by those hieroglyphic marks, had written out on his body a complete theory of the heavens and the earth, and a mystical treatise on the art of attaining truth; so that Queequeg in his own proper person was a riddle to unfold; a wondrous work in one volume; but whose mysteries not even himself could read, though his own live heart beat against them; and these mysteries were therefore destined in the end to moulder away with the living parchment whereon they were inscribed, and so be unsolved to the last.

Somewhat later in the novel it is discovered that the lifebuoys on the Pequod, which are sealed casks, have been warped by the sun so as to be useless. It occurs to Queequeg that his coffin might, if the lid were sealed on, substitute admirably for the ruined buoys, and so the coffin takes its place on the ship as a life-preserver. No more is heard of it until the Epilogue. After the Pequod has been rammed by Moby Dick and has disappeared under the sea, Ishmael is saved by its means, and in such a manner as to make it almost appear, when he is picked up by the Rachel, as if he had been resurrected from his own coffin. And the coffin itself is a very special one. It belonged to his friend Queequeg, one of the noblest savages in literature—a primitive prince whose whole way of life is based, not on enmity to nature, as with Ahab, but on harmony with nature. And we know from Queequeg's whole life, as Melville gives it to us, that he represents a kind of instinctive charity and adjustment to the world that is the antithesis of Ahab's madness. To recapture the full flavour of Queequeg's moral implications, we have to go back to Chapter X:

> As I sat there in that lonely room; the fire burning low, in that mild stage when, after its first intensity has warmed the air, it then only glows to be looked at; the evening shades and phantoms gathering round the casements, and peering in upon us silent, solitary twain; the storm booming without in solemn swells; I began to be sensible of strange feelings. I felt a melting in me. No more my splintered heart and maddened hand were turned against the wolfish world. This soothing savage had redeemed it. There he sat, his very indifference speaking a nature in which there lurked no civilized hypocrisies, and bland deceits. Wild he was; a very sight of sights to see; yet I began to feel myself mysteriously drawn towards him.

What have we noticed particularly about Ishmael's survival is that it happens, in fact, virtually through Queequeg's agency. By virtue of the carving on the lid which duplicates the tattooing on Queequeg's body, the coffin stands in proxy for the savage himself. And we should remember what the design represented: '. . . a complete theory of the heavens and the earth, and a mystical treatise on the art of attaining truth.' Although not obtrusive, this symbolism is nevertheless straight-forward and clear. Ahab himself represents hatred of creation — an extremity of madness, symptoms of which Ishmael had begun to show when he took to the sea for a cure. He is saved, or cured, by an acceptance of nature, of the earth and the heavens. This is what the hieroglyphics on Queequeg's coffin lid symbolize, and Ishmael's physical survival by its means stands also for his spiritual recovery.

Moby Dick is, then, Melville's great attempt to create order in a universe in which a break-down of the polarity between good and evil is threatened. This threat comes from Ahab, whose hatred of creation is the symptom, or perhaps the consequence, of that democratic disillusionment with the universe I have spoken of — that resentment of the spirit's betrayal of matter, and of God's betrayal of the world. In so far as Melville's own thought is to be equated with any particular person's, it is with Ishmael's. Ishmael represents Melville's resistance against the temptation to follow Ahab which was so powerful for him; he represents Melville's hold on the world of reality and of nature. But as Melville plunged almost immediately into the writing of *Pierre* when he had finsihed *Moby Dick*, the sanity and grace that had shaped the earlier of the two books was to vanish for good.

5. Epilogue

Conrad Aiken

[*Moby-Dick* and the Puritan Dream]

If in this sense Hawthorne was the only commentator on transcendental individualism, and the one analyst and chronicler of the final phases of the evolution of the Puritan passion for freedom of conscience, he was also the only link between the Concord group and the writer who carried farthest and deepest that perilous frontier of mystic consciousness which had always been the Puritan's fiercest concern: Herman Melville. *Moby Dick* was dedicated to Hawthorne, and it was written while Hawthorne and Melville were neighbors in Pittsfield. Without any question the greatest book which has come out of New England, and one of the very greatest works of prose fiction ever written in any language, it is also the final and perfect finial to the Puritan's desperate three-century-long struggle with the problem of evil. Hunted from consciousness into the unconscious, and in effect beyond space and time, magnificently sublimated so that it becomes not one issue but all issues, a superb and almost unanalyzable matrix of universal symbolism, the white whale is the Puritan's central dream of delight and terror, the all-

From *The Collected Criticism of Conrad Aiken from 1916 to the Present: A Reviewer's ABC* (New York: Meridian Books, Inc., 1958), pp. 91-92 hating and all-loving, all-creating and all-destroying implacable god, whose magnetism none can escape, and who must be faced and fought with on the frontier of awareness with the last shred of one's moral courage and one's moral despair. Man against God? Is the principle of things, at last, to be seen as essentially evil? And re-deemable only by war *à l'outrance?* Impossible, at any rate, to sur-render; one's freedom to feel toward it what one will, whether hatred or love, must be preciously preserved. One must grapple with it, and alone, and in darkness, no matter whether it lead to a death throe or to an all-consuming love.

Melville, writing to Hawthorne about this extraordinary book, which was destined for half a century to be considered just a good romance for boys, likened himself to one who strips off the layers of consciousness as one might strip off the layers of an onion, and added that he had come at last to the central core. And indeed to all intents he had; when a year later, at the age of thirty-three, he published *Pierre*, he had really finished his voyage. And he had car-ried William Blackstone with him to such strange borderlands as that bold explorer of Rhode Island never dreamed of. Perhaps it is worth noting that Melville himself denied that *Moby Dick* had any allegorical intention—if only to point out that the denial can really have no meaning. *Mardi* was quite obviously allegorical; allegory and parable came almost instinctively to the hands of a group so vitally concerned with moral and religious matters, and as a "form" it very likely seemed no more artifical or unusual to Hawthorne or Melville than that, say, of a poem: it was something which played with meaning and which gave out meanings on many different levels, and that was the end of it. . . .

William Faulkner

[Moby-Dick: "Golgotha of the Heart"]

I think that the book which I put down with the unqualified thought « I wish I had written that » is Moby Dick. The Greek-like simplicity of it: a man of forceful character driven by his somber nature and his bleak heritage, bent on his own destruction and dragging his immediate world down with him with a despotic and utter disregard of them as individuals; the fine point to which the various natures caught [and passive as though with a foreknowledge of unalterable doom] in the fatality of his blind course are swept— a sort of Golgotha of the heart become immutable as bronze in the sonority of its plunging ruin; all timeless phase: the sea. And the symbol of their doom: a White Whale. There's a death for a man, now; none of your patient pasturage for little grazing beasts you can't even see with the naked eye. There's magic in the very word. A White Whale. White is a grand word, like a crash of massed trumpets; and leviathan himself has a kind of placid blundering majesty in his name. And then put them together!!! A death for Achilles, and the divine maidens of Patmos to mourn him, to harp white-handed sorrow on their golden hair.

From Chicago *Tribune,* "Books," July 6, 1927, p. 12. Reprinted in Hans Burgert, "William Faulkner on *Moby-Dick:* An Early Letter," *Studi Americani,* IX (1963), 371-375.

Hart Crane

At Melville's Tomb

Often beneath the wave, wide from this ledge
The dice of drowned men's bones he saw bequeath
An embassy. Their numbers as he watched,
Beat on the dusty shore and were obscured.

And wrecks passed without sound of bells,
The calyx of death's bounty giving back
A scattered chapter, livid hieroglyph.
The portent wound in corridors of shells.

Then in the circuit calm of one vast coil,
Its lashings charmed and malice reconciled,
Frosted eyes there were that lifted altars;
And silent answers crept across the stars.

Compass, quadrant and sextant contrive
No farther tides . . . High in the azure steeps
Monody shall not wake the mariner.
This fabulous shadow only the sea keeps.

From *Complete Poems & Selected Letters & Prose of Hart Crane* by Hart Crane, p. 104. Permission by Liveright, Copyright 1933, 1958, 1966 by Liveright Publishing Corp. Publishers, New York.